1986-1

THE BUSINESS GUIDE TO SMALL COMPUTERS

Lawrence Calmus

Perelman/Calmus of Los Angeles, California

McGraw-Hill Book Company

New York St. Louis San Francisco Auckland Bogotá Hamburg
Johannesburg London Madrid Mexico Montreal New Delhi
Panama Paris São Paulo Singapore Sydney Tokyo Toronto

eI 8⁴
7-9-84

Library of Congress Cataloging in Publication Data

Calmus, Lawrence.
  The business guide to small computers.

  Includes index.
  1. Business—Data processing.   2. Microcomputers.
I. Title.
HF5548.2.C237   1983   001.64′04′024658   82-10080
ISBN 0-07-009662-7

  2 3 4 5 6 7 8 9 0   DOCDOC   8 9 8 7 6 5 4 3

ISBN 0-07-009662-7

The editors for this book were William R. Newton and Dorick J. Byard, the designer was Elliot Epstein, and the production supervisor was Sally Fliess. It was set in Souvenir by Santype-Byrd.

Printed and bound by R. R. Donnelley & Sons Company.

This book is dedicated to
AARON *and* JANE CALMUS,
who taught me the tools of learning.

ABOUT THE AUTHOR

Lawrence Calmus has been involved with computers for nearly 20 years. His application programs have been used in all areas of business, from banking to retail sales organizations. Since the start of his career, the author has been involved with and interested in the design of computer systems for non-computer-oriented people. He has designed programmed learning courses for use with elementary school children and has overseen many second to third generation mainframe processor conversions.

For the past 3 years he has implemented systems utilizing Apple II, Z80, and 8080 CP/M-based processors. He has successfully developed and implemented computer systems in such areas as personnel management, word processing, management information, and financial accounting. Currently he is a partner of PERELMAN/CALMUS, which designs, configures, and implements small computers for business. He and his associates are also involved in the development and marketing of business application packages for use on small computers. As consultants, their clients range from small businesses setting up their primary electronic data processing center to Fortune 500 companies utilizing small computers as distributed processing centers.

CONTENTS

PREFACE

This guide is an account of systems analysis for the business use of a small computer. In the last few years microprocessors have made the computer small, personable, and friendly. The turn-key system has arrived, and any establishment that has an electric typewriter can have a small computer. Fortunately or unfortunately, a small computer differs from an electric typewriter in all respects. Although the new computers are comparatively easy to operate, take up little room, and are inexpensive, they are also incredibly powerful. The impact a small computer can have on the business environment is enormous.

Today's small computer is as powerful as yesterday's computer. This means that all the accoutrements of electronic data processing that occupied a business organization in the past are still with us. The advent of the microprocessor chip has shrunk the computer room to the corner of a desk. However, the need for support material and personnel, systems analysts, programmers, operations managers, and data librarians hasn't shrunk. In fact, of this entire list only the programmer has been replaced. Packaged software is an efficient and economical solution to the data processing personnel problem of in-house development. However, all the remaining functions still exist and must be performed if a small computer is to be used to its full potential.

This book is a work and procedures manual to take you step-by-step through the installation of a small computer.

A small computer can be compared to a fine automobile. It will travel far and fast, but only if it has the roads to travel on. Without a network of roads a car is unable to operate at its peak of efficiency. A small computer without clearly defined systems of information flow is unable to effectively traverse the business environment.

This book will enable both current and first-time users to chart the paths of the work flow. A glossary has been provided for both the text and for commonly used computer terms not covered by the book. Techniques for determining your data processing needs are detailed. An exploration of the underlying principles of computer hardware and software will enable the reader to choose equipment to satisfy the system's requirements. And finally, daily operation of the projected system is covered so that the final phase of implementation will leave you with a fully functioning system. By working through the steps described in the text, the reader will not only implement a new system but will also create a work and procedures manual for the system.

The ideas and views presented in this book are neither new nor original. They are, however, the expression of computer common sense that has been accumulated by many people over many years. One individual whose human common sense helped in the preparation of this manuscript is Mr. Morton Schaeffer.

Lawrence Calmus

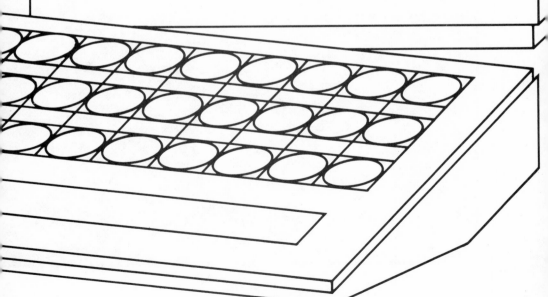

1 INTRODUC-TION TO SYSTEMS ANALYSIS

1 INTRODUCTION TO SYSTEMS ANALYSIS

Provide a point of view from which to describe your electronic data processing needs. Make tools available to begin the process of analysis. Break down your business activity in order to identify the elements in your work flow.

I. SYSTEMS ANALYSIS—A POINT OF VIEW

II. DETERMINE THE ELEMENTS
1. Context: Where does the business element come from?
2. Work Flow: What is done to the element?
3. The Black Box: Am I asking enough different questions?

4. Five W's and an H: Who, what, when, where, why, and how?

III. DEFINE THE WORK FLOW
1. The Theory of Extremes: What is the worst case?
2. Common Activities: What areas of business practice are being considered?

SYSTEMS ANALYSIS—A POINT OF VIEW

Computers are a tool. To use them properly it is necessary to know their place in the business system, and the systems point of view is to look at the interrelationship of parts rather than the parts themselves.

Obviously, an object may be a system at one level and a discrete element at another. The heart, for example, is a part of the circulatory system, while at another level the heart itself is a system made up of different elements: muscle tissue, nerves, veins, arteries. The field of view and the orientation of the observer determine whether an object is seen as a system or as a part.

Systems analysis by definition is concerned with analyzing the interrelationship of parts—it defines a system. The clue to an understanding of systems analysis is that it views objects from a dynamic perspective. A tree, for example, could be seen as a static collection of separate parts. It is made up of roots, trunk, branches, leaves, sap, bark, and cellulose, and defining a tree in these terms can be helpful when it is necessary to identify and classify it. We can then describe a tree by those data elements we have collected. However, if we wish to look at how the parts make up a particular tree, we would also look at their relationship to each other.

The job of the systems analyst is to identify the effective factors and describe their relationship. Systems analysis is a complex field of study with many highly trained practitioners. The purpose of this book is to make you aware of the pattern of thinking used by analysts and computer professionals. The more familiar you become with computer common sense, the more you can utilize the new tools of the small computer age.

A small computer is powerful, but it is not the entire business. Its utilization always requires some preliminary analysis of the environment in which it will be used. Many first-time computer users are so impressed by the magic of the machine, they have an image of a box with a removable lid into which everything is poured. Then, by pushing a few buttons, the results will come out. This is a tragically false impression that has resulted in underutilization of computers and anger on the part of users. The point is that installing and making use of a computer requires planning. Luckily, all businesses have some resident experts on the nature of that business: the people doing the work. As computers become friendlier, they interact with the people using them by asking questions. Systems analysis, computer common sense, makes the questions understandable and points out the direction in which the answers lie.

In journalism, reporters look for the who, what, when, where, why, and how of a story; that way they are sure of covering it completely. A story written with all the elements has a flow to it that seems quite natural, and any area of business treated in the same way will yield the same result: a description of the flow of activity.

Regardless of the orientation of a business, i.e., profit, nonprofit, self-aggrandizement, or research, the survival of the business is dependent on activity. So, like journalism, the first task of systems analysis is the isolation and description of the main activity of a business. A major tool for doing this is a description of the obvious.

DETERMINE THE ELEMENTS

A large, decentralized corporation knows this and provides extensive paper trails (hopefully) for its employees to follow. A relatively small, centralized business with less than 200 employees run by 1 to 5 people will often rely on the knowledge of the leaders to ensure the business flow. And if the particular boss can't keep up with everything, then there is the indispensable assistant who handles all the details.

It is just those details that need to be isolated and described if a computer is to be inserted into the business activity. And it is just those details that may be jealously guarded because of the power they bring to the individual. Chapter 2 discusses some specific techniques for gaining this information and organizing it for the computer.

Information is the life's blood of business. It may take the form of a letter to a supplier, an invoice to a dealer, an inventory tag, an amount of money to be paid out, an amount of money to be paid in, or any of the thousand and one things that make up the daily activities of a business. And a computer is a tool for making sure that no matter how heavy the flow, the business remains strong and healthy.

Systems analysis charts this flow for the same reason that a river is charted before a shipping service is launched. There may be sandbars that can be eliminated, alternate routes that could speed up or slow down the traffic, way stations to test progress, or unfriendly natives to be avoided.

Context: Where does the business element come from?

No matter how large or small a company may be, it will fall somewhere on a line between centralized and decentralized. In other words, it has a certain style to its operation. This style, this manner of doing business, is an integral part of the system. It is important to determine the attitude toward information on the part of the operating powers.

A centralized company often sees itself as paternal and all-knowing, providing firm guidelines wherever needed. Therefore, detailed information must be made available to a central control and acted on, and the result must be communicated to the periphery. The concern with this type of operation is that a bottleneck can occur, and business could come to a halt.

A decentralized organization often sees itself as a collection of smaller entities, the whole of which is greater than the sum of its parts. Here, information is acted upon as it occurs. This necessitates that the knowledge of decision requirements be dispersed and available at individual decision points. Information is delegated. Extensive summary information must be given to a coordinating control, and up-to-date status information must be made available to all decision points.

Let us take a one-person business, where the individual alone sells property and carries the mortgages. A computer is needed to keep track of the monthly payments by principal and interest. A centralized system would lean toward a full accounting system with the individual making all the necessary decisions. A decentralized system would keep track of the mortgage payments but give summary payment sheets to the accounting service that takes care of the books. It is important to keep in mind that an attitude is being described. Computers, amoral machines that they are, will work for anyone.

Work Flow: What is done to the element?

Work flow is such an understandable phrase that we are unaware of its meaning. We no longer look at its constituent parts—work and flow. Work is one thing; flow is another thing. A description of each thing gives meaning to the phrase. Computers are by their nature hairsplitters.

Most of us see the words "ignorant" and "stupid" interchangeably. But "ignorant" means "not aware of," while "stupid" means "difficulty in learning." Most computers are not stupid; they're ignorant.

The more you can tell a computer, the better it performs. Computer performance requires that:

1. You have loads of things to tell it.

2. It has the capacity to absorb all these things.

Small computers have less room for details than large computers. It's the details that determine a computer's efficiency.

Work, by definition, is something that effects something else. Carpenters work on wood to build houses. Joiners work on wood to build furniture. Accountants work on figures to build businesses. Secretaries work on letters to build communication.

Take the example of the work involved in sharpening a wooden pencil. The secretary or accountant may look at the tip, decide it's too short, sharpen it in a pencil sharpener, and go back to work. The designer of a wooden pencil would look at the same event, but have other considerations. In manufacturing a wooden pencil that can be sharpened by the user, the designer would ask:

1. What was the minimum diameter of the lead before it broke?

2. What is the average pressure on a sharpened point?

3. What kind of wood sharpens easily?

4. How can the wood be bonded together to hold the lead?

Same problem, different points of view, and so different questions. The problem of sharpening a pencil has a different work flow for the user than it does for the designer.

Perhaps the easiest way to approach work flow is from the point of view of the black box.

The Black Box: Am I asking enough different questions?

A black box is a device that does "what you want it to do." Whatever you want, it will do it—you don't need to know how it does it; you just know that it does it.

When you walk into a store to buy a black box, the first question the salesperson asks is, "What do you want it to do?" You might reply:

1. I want it to make ice cream.

2. I want it to sharpen pencils.

3. I want it to do my accounting.

4. I want it to type my letters.

Answer number 1, "I want it to make ice cream," might find the salesperson asking, "Do you want it to make one flavor or many flavors?" Answer number 2, "I want it to sharpen pencils," might find the salesperson asking, "Do you want the black box to sharpen pencils or to make pencils that can be sharpened?" The more details you can give, the better the salesperson can help you find the correct black box.

At a primary level, the computer is just another black box, one that is designed to fit the work flow. Remember, a black box is always in the middle. It is never the beginning and never the end. Something always has to go into the black box and something always has to come out. Black boxes take "input," do something, and give "output." Black boxes that make ice cream require milk, flavoring, cold, and energy in order to yield ice cream. Leaving out one essential ingredient will give a different result. Ice cream makers don't yield yogurt, even though they are both milk products. Accounting systems do not prepare answers for "what if" questions; that requires a modeling system.

In order to determine which black box is best for your company, someone has to determine in detail what your company will put into the box and what your company expects to get out of it.

Five W's and an H: Who, what, when, where, why, and how?

To determine the company details that feed a particular black box, use an adaptation of the journalistic approach to a story. In journalism, who, what, when, where, why, and how organize and describe the facts of the news. In systems analysis, asking these questions in the order where, what, how, when, who, and why organizes and describes the elements of the work flow. By placing an element in context, we develop a systematic view of the business.

One probable and valid result of this may be the recognition that a computer will not enhance the work flow of the business. Or, it may point up the need for a larger system than was originally surmised.

Any element can be placed in a system by asking six questions:

1. Where does the element come from?

2. What is done to the element?

3. How is the element manipulated?

4. When is the element acted upon?

5. Who gets the element after this stage of the process?

6. Why is the element necessary?

WHERE DOES THE ELEMENT COME FROM?

This question can help determine the element's identity—a piece of paper with the number 5 on it from a salesperson has a good chance of being a quantity order. A letter from a salesperson has a good chance of being customer relations material. Simple? Of course. The point is that determining the origin enables you to start delineating the decisions.

A shipping order, by definition, must affect inventory. If it doesn't, then something is wrong. Most errors in computer systems are not the result of complex manipulations, but rather something so simple no one bothered to make a note of it.

On December 31, 1980, at midnight, a major national computer time-sharing network went down; that is, it stopped functioning. For some hours, large corporations were unable to conduct business until the problem was fixed. The corporations considered the lost time to be valued in the billions of dollars and threatened suit against the computer corporation that maintained the network. The magnitude of the occurrence, while not catastrophic, was major.

The cause was extremely simple. Computer systems keep track of the number of days in a year and verify that the user has signed on with the correct date. In other words, February 3 would be the 34th day out of 365 days in a year. 1980 was a leap year. Somebody neglected to tell the computer that there were 366 days that year.

So, at midnight, December 31, 1980, when people tried to sign on, the computer interpreted it as the 366th day, and things didn't match up. An error condition was not accounted for, and the computer system could neither do anything nor indicate what was wrong, all because everybody knows that February has 29 days in a leap year. Everybody, that is, except the computer system.

Somewhere, someone neglected to ask the following:

Question: Where does the date come from?"

Answer: "A built-in-day-counter calendar."

Question: "That's interesting, but does it keep track of leap years?"

WHAT IS DONE TO THE ELEMENT?

An element will not be acted upon all the time. When it is acted upon, we need to know exactly what is done to it. This can be a very hazy area for many people. They know exactly what they're doing and find it so routine and simple that they assume everyone else knows what they do. Chapter 2 provides some techniques for uncovering what is done.

A common problem that grows out of this area is that of processed information. It comes to light when the system is installed and the first reports have been generated. Someone then asks, "Where's the breakdown of totals of items ordered, by salesperson?" and it's not there because someone neglected to inform the supplier of the computer system that this was a necessary subtotal to track.

Finding out what is done to the element also identifies its compatibility with a particular section of the system. Many an organization has an individual who will act as both secretary and bookkeeper. And, although a computer can perform certain of these functions, small computer systems do not do them in parallel, the way they occur in real life. An individual may take an order, update inventory, prepare the invoice, post information to a ledger, and type out a letter to go with the order before moving on to the next order. Small computer systems are rarely integrated in that style.

HOW IS THE ELEMENT MANIPULATED?

This question attempts to define the formulas of action. The totals of "items ordered, by salesperson" is kept in an order log in one company and in a salesperson's log in another. Some companies determine their foreign price list by multiplying their domestic price list by 110 percent. Other companies assign foreign prices by the judgment of the owner. It can be a great help to know how the data element is manipulated.

Let's look at another area of business where computers are extensively used—word processing. A manufacturer may announce a new product or process at a technical convention. The talk may be written up to be handed out to participants and also to be made available to the news media. Later on, as the new item enters the market place, data sheets are prepared.

It is very helpful if, in the original presentation material, the new data is indexed in such a way that it is easily obtainable for sales support material. There are few things as frustrating as preparing material and then being told, "Oh, we always take the synopsis paragraph from the initial lectures as our data sheets." That's assuming the company is systematic enough to have a method.

One of the great boons of word processing is the ability to call up *boiler plate material*, which is a series of standard sentences or statements that usually appear in most company literature and that the secretary adds as a matter of course. "Usually" and "most" are the operative words here. What is there about a particular piece of literature that determines whether or not a boiler plate sentence or paragraph is added? How is the literature manipulated to arrive at its finished form?

WHEN IS THE ELEMENT ACTED UPON?

Some things have to be done right away, and other things don't. There are two parts to this question:

1. What's the latest this can be done without disrupting anything?

2. What has to be done before this is worked on?

A well-designed computer system will operate sequentially in the style of what has to be done first, second, third, and so on. No computer system can determine all possible timings and compensate for them. No matter how fast a computer may process information, the computer is only part of the flow of information.

Systems analysis means looking at the entire operation. A computer functioning as a word processor may retype a letter in 2 minutes. The question you have to ask is "How long does it take to get approval of the draft by the originator?" If Ms. Smith wants the letter mailed that evening and she's only available to review letters in the morning, the effective turnaround time for the system is 24 hours.

Keep in mind that while Ms. Smith is utilizing the computer for word processing, Mr. Jones may need to generate invoices. A computer system is like a group of kids on a hike—it's as fast as its slowest member. In other words, do you want multiple access or single access to the machinery of your system. Depending on the sophistication of the small computer, it is possible to have more than one person use the machine at one time. This is known as a *multiuser machine*, which means that there is more than one terminal attached to the machine.

WHO GETS THE ELEMENT AFTER THIS STAGE OF THE PROCESS?

The person or group who receives the element, whether it be an object or a piece of data, has some expectations. The packaging department of a small manufacturer, for example, expects to receive finished goods. An accountant expects to get certain types of reports in a certain way.

Determining people's expectations makes it possible to describe the existing system. Some areas of the system may operate as described, and others may not. Because people are the crucial element in any business, it is important to understand their needs.

A businessperson may need sales information on a timely basis, rather than an analysis of sales on a periodic cycle. Timely reports require timely updates. This means that data entry must be simple and available.

Computers have voracious appetites, and in order to get information out, information must be fed in. If up-to-date information is desired, then this expectation ripples backward through the system. Systems are dynamic entities. Asking "Who gets the element?" is inextricably linked to "Where does the element come from?" Where, what, how, when, who, and why are all parts of the same puzzle.

Systems analysis uses "who" as the keystone of a system. Who gets the element determines everything else. "Who" determines the layout of a system. Small computers by design are oriented toward the "who" of a system.

The small computer is the least expensive element of a business system; personnel is the most expensive. A good business system is designed to take advantage of the talents of the people involved.

WHY IS THE ELEMENT NECESSARY?

An element may be a necessary by-product of the business flow. It may also be necessary in and of itself. An invoice is a good example of how to use this question.

An invoice is generated for the sale of a product or service. One copy of the invoice should go to the buyer. At least one copy is a necessary by-product. It seems obvious that one copy should go to the seller. But let's see if that's the only answer. The seller has a copy stored in the computer system and does not necessarily require individual sheets (*hard copies*) of every invoice.

Another possibility is that a small business is part of a larger organization, and hard copies are used for data verification. If the volume of invoices is great and data verification is essential, then it may be worthwhile to use two-part paper. If the volume is small, it may be simpler to photocopy the invoices and send them over.

A third alternative is that all departments have computer systems and information is transferred from computer system to computer system. The point is that just because a business has always produced multiple copies of an element does not mean that the computer system has to slavishly copy the old system.

DEFINE THE WORK FLOW

Having identified the data element, the next step is to chart its passage through the system. To do this properly, we need to account for all possible permutations of the element's flow. This would be a horrendous task if it had to be done from the ground up.

The Theory of Extremes: What is the worst case?

Fortunately, the theory of extremes comes to our rescue; it says that once you've found either the largest or smallest example of an element, all other examples line up behind it.

Applying the theory of extremes to the idea of weeks, we realize that the extreme case of a week is a minimum and a maximum of 7 days. A week has to have 7 days, not 6, 5, 4, or 8, 9, 10.

On the other hand, the maximum number of clients a law firm will ever handle at one time is 100. Therefore, the extreme case for current clients is 100. In this instance, any computer system that can handle 100 clients can handle 99, 98, and so on. But it cannot, without modification, handle even 1 more; 101 is out.

A mail-order retail business may need to generate address labels with first and last names. The largest last name is 12 characters long, and they are willing to use one initial and a period for the first name. Therefore, the extreme case for the work flow is 14 positions.

A business requires a payroll system that handles 100 employees who earn individual commission checks that could, in rare cases, total $20,000 each in one month. A black box that prints checks no greater than $5000 at a time is not the right system for a firm that could pay $20,000 in individual monthly commissions. Keep in mind that even if the printer is capable of printing higher numbers or if the computer could do it but changes would have to be made, this black box is not the right black box.

By listing the extremes you guarantee the median. It is always possible to adjust the extremes toward the middle. It is not always possible to expand the middle toward the extremes. By accounting for the largest, smallest, greatest, or least occurrence of an item, you ensure the system's ability to cope with the work flow. And the description of the work element and its flow make up the things a computer system should be told. That way, the right black box is the one that meets your list of extremes.

Any business activity has two parts: the element being worked on and its movement through the business environment. The element can be a thing or a service. If we look at the work element as a thing, it can be described by its physical result: typing ten 2-page letters results in 20 pages and 10 envelopes. Looking at the work element as a service, it can be described by its conclusion: answering 10 customers' telephone calls that average 2 minutes each results in 20 minutes on the phone.

Describing the work element in some physically measurable way provides the first half of the strategy for defining extremes. The second half is determined by describing the movement. The movement of an element can be described by how long it takes and when it takes place.

"How long" plus "when" will give the total time to complete an activity. For example, it may take only 2 minutes to enter the day's inventory numbers in the ledger. But they can be entered only at the end of the day's work. An inventory clerk that comes in 4 hours early to enter the day's numbers would not be considered sensible.

Yet many people will judge a black box by how fast it can print a line. It may have to wait 4 hours to get the information and then take 30 minutes to process that information. Remember, system time is more than just computer operating time.

To determine "when" something takes place, ask three things:

1. Does it take place before anything else?

2. Does it take place during anything else?

3. Does it take place after anything else?

Question 3 determines what has to be completed. If a secretary has to type 10 letters, the first draft has to be created by the originator before the typing can begin.

Question 2 determines the limits of parallel activity. A secretary may type letters and answer the phone at the same time. However, a secretary cannot be expected to type letters, answer the phone, and take dictation at the same time.

Question 1 determines priority. A secretary who has to deliver 10 typed letters in 5 minutes may ask someone else to answer the phone.

Common Activities: What areas of business practice are being considered?

In summary, systems analysis is the practice of looking at particular business situations and identifying common areas of activity. This is done by defining the reasons for installing a black box according to some general areas of business activity. These are usually:

1. Secretarial typing, called *word processing*

2. Filing and Selection, called *data base management*

3. Ledger activity, called *general accounting*

4. "What if" questions, called *electronic spread sheets*

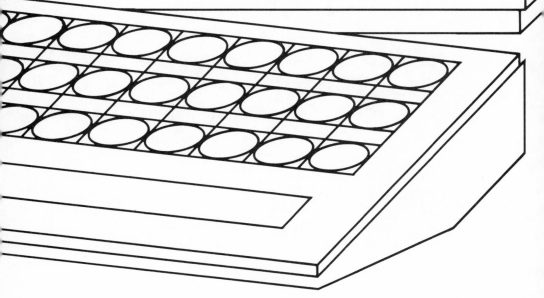

2 ANALYZING THE COMPANY

2 ANALYZING THE COMPANY

Provide a coherent description of how your company currently works on a day-to-day basis. Design a new system that reflects your company's operating needs and your present and future requirements.

I. FINDING OUT WHO YOU ARE—THE REAL COMPANY

II. GATHERING INFORMATION
1. Interviewing: Who really does what?
2. Collecting Samples: What things are needed to keep the place running smoothly?
3. Making Lists: Did I forget something?

4. Determining Timings: How long does it take and what order is it done in?

III. ORGANIZING THE INFORMATION
   1. Input-Output (I/O) Descriptions: What does the system expect from us, and what do we expect from the system—exactly?
   2. Procedure Descriptions: How does it all fit together?

FINDING OUT WHO YOU ARE—THE REAL COMPANY

Perhaps the hardest task of analysis is that of describing what is rather than what is believed. Inscribed upon the Delphic oracle 2000 years ago were the words "Know thyself." In the business world it is a task of analysis to describe what is happening, what people think is happening, and what people would like to happen. And a large part of analyzing a system is separating the gathered information into those three categories.

Once you have determined what is happening you will have a description of where you are, a benchmark or standard by which to chart the future growth of your business. Determining what people think is happening provides you with a means of identifying problems and isolating areas that need adjustment. Separating out what people would like to happen enables you to design your new system so that it is *user-friendly*; that is, it is easy to work with because it is designed to people's needs rather than forcing them to adapt to an unfamiliar system. These three parts even apply to setting up a new, first-time business system. The only difference is that rather than using your own business as the benchmark you identify an existing business and use it as your standard to imitate, adapt, or improve. After all, it is axiomatic of analytical thinking and deductive reasoning that we start with a given and work backward. Even if that given is a dream, a nonexistent desire, the purpose and value of systems analysis is to provide a map to lead us to our goal.

GATHERING INFORMATION

Systems analysis has developed certain methods to create its maps, its descriptions of how a business gets from here to there. There are two basic types of tools used in systems analysis. The first group includes anything that helps you gather information: interviewing people, collecting samples, making lists, recording timings. The second group of tools includes anything that helps you organize your information: flowcharts, narrative descriptions, decision tables, timing constraints.

The trick, if there is a trick to efficient systems anaylsis, is to start at the end and work toward that well-defined target.

It is essential that you know where you want to go and that you state your goal clearly. It is, for example, not the same thing to say, "I want to computerize my system," and "I want a more efficient system." That first group of tools, anything that helps you gather information, will enable you to describe your system. The tools from the second group, those that organize your information, will help you to make certain value judgments about your system.

Once you have described your system, you can describe where you want to go and then determine how to get there. The process is similar to going on a trip. First you unfold a map and determine where you are and where you want to go. Then you choose the way of traveling that best meets your personal needs. You may want to get there quickly and so choose to fly. Or you may want to see the countryside and so choose to go by road. Systems analysis is like that map; first you have to identify where you are and where you want to be. Then you can figure out the best road to travel.

Interviewing: Who really does what?

All businesses have one thing in common—they involve people. Interviewing provides information on how things are operating. Interviewing also provides information on how people would like things to happen. These two aspects of interviewing provide information on how things are done and the attitude of those who are doing it.

It must be made clear to the people being interviewed and remain clear in the mind of the interviewer that the function of the interview is to help people, not to draw up a plan at the expense of the individual.

The goal of an interview is the description of three areas of an individual's work:

1. What is done—operations

2. Where the work comes from—input

3. Where the work goes—output

In defining operations, the interviewer probes the following to answer the question, "What is being done?"

- Who does what, when, and how?
- Where and why?
- How long?
- What are the ideas and feelings that experienced people have about what they are doing?
- What are the rules, written and unwritten, that govern the work done?

In defining input, the interviewer probes the following to answer the question, "Where does the work come from?"

- Who gives it?
- What are they giving?
- When did they give it?
- Why is it given?
- How do you get it?

In defining output, the interviewer probes the following to answer the question, "Where does the work go?"

- Who gets it?
- What do they get?
- When do they get it?
- Why do they get it?
- How do they get it?

The stuff of systems analysis is information and the generalized questions of each of the above areas will need to be defined and redefined by the interviewer. After all, when someone is asked about the output of their work, the answer to the question "where is it going" depends on its condition. A correctly filled out form, for example, goes on to the next step in the process; an incorrectly filled out form may either be returned or go to a special error-handling section. The whole point of the interview is to fill in and delineate all the little things that one normally takes for granted. Good interviewers ask the same question many different ways to be sure that they unearth a complete description of what they're after.

In conducting an interview, consider the following:

1. Know what is being sought and tell the person being interviewed why it is being done.

2. Schedule interviews in advance. If there is a great deal of information to be gathered, try to schedule several short interviews rather than one long one.

3. Start at the top and work down. There are two reasons for this. One, it's easier to start with a broad general view and then fill in the details. Two, if you are not part of the managerial structure of the organization you are analyzing, it helps to have a manager introduce you to a subordinate.

4. Try to speak to different people about the same thing.

5. Do the homework. Know what the people you're interviewing are supposed to be doing. Then when you talk to them you can determine both what they do and how their personalities affect what they are doing.

6. Be flexible in dealing with people. If asking questions isn't working, try getting them to discuss their feelings about the work.

7. Pay attention. You must listen not only to what is being said but also to how it is said.

8. Allow people time. Remember, in an interview you are there to get information, not to talk about your ideas.

9. Document what you are doing. Use a tape recorder, take notes, draw diagrams, and get samples if possible.

10. At the conclusion of the interview summarize information while the person is still there. Make sure that you understand what you've been told.

11. On your own time determine if you've found out what is needed. You may need to go back for another interview, or you may have to go elsewhere for the information.

Collecting Samples: What things are needed
to keep the place running smoothly?

There are two parts to collecting samples. One part is to get a sample of all the things that are done. For example, if different forms are filled out, it is helpful to have a copy of these forms and indications of what is done to them. The other part is to sample the work that is done. In other words, to record the activities involved in the task. It is better to do this work sampling at random times according to a predetermined set of categories. By work sampling, you are trying to determine the individual actions that make up the work flow. Independent observation is a check against information obtained during the process of interviewing.

Observations should be gathered at random intervals in as unobtrusive a manner as possible. The greatest obstacle to successful analysis is people's unwillingness to change; their suspicion of something new. Often the gathered information is compiled and used as a means of communicating with the people involved. Written or verbal comments on this information may be asked for. In the world of small computers and friendly systems, the results of sampling information are of great value as a way of involving people in the new system.

Taking a work sample can be as simple as looking at broad categories of activity, such as telephone time, reading, writing, and talking. Or it may be more specifically oriented to the type of work done, such as consulting parts directories, filling in names and addresses, creating new purchase order numbers. The specificity of the categories will be determined by the work level being reviewed. If the clerical functions of the secretary are being observed, the categories can be determined from the job description. If the job description doesn't exist, then this provides information for its creation. A manager, on the other hand, spends time in more general ways. The object of the exercise is to ascertain who is doing what and why. And at this point in the analysis it is inappropriate to make any value judgments.

Making Lists: Did I forget something?

Having gathered the information, the simple act of listing what has been collected is a powerful tool. Listing everything helps to determine the completeness of the data collection. The point of making a list is to draw attention to what is not covered, eliminate duplications, and draw attention to areas of common activity.

The first step involves cross-referencing the input list with the output list and making sure that what is not accounted for on either list is covered in the procedures list. Second, the act of listing information helps define the individual parts, making them amenable to shifting and changing (to see how they can be changed). Third, lists begin to uncover redundancies and draw attention to interfacing areas of activity. After all, if document A appears both on the input list and on the output list, it is necessary to ask if anything was done to it during the processing phase. Drawing up lists should include people and equipment and in both cases should state what they do and what they are capable of doing.

Determining Timings: How long does
it take and what order is it done in?

Most people are very poor judges of how long it takes to do something. The importance of timing is as an aid to scheduling. It is not enough to know that a person can do their work in an 8-hour day.

Changing a system may require that the order of work be changed around. However, the order can only be changed if all the necessary pieces are ready on time for the next step. As obvious as this sounds, it is often ignored when a business installs a small computer. The small desk top computer is not only friendly but also powerful. And its very efficiency in producing information can create a bottleneck that will defeat the purpose of the computer installation.

Timings are done to determine both duration and priority; that is, how long something takes and what order it is done in. Timings can be determined in a number of ways. The simplest way is to use a watch and observe an action from start to finish. It is important to time a complete cycle and to differentiate between different parts of the same cycle. If, for example, a secretary is asked to type a letter, the time it takes to create the typed letter can be just the time it takes to type it or it may include the time it takes to find the correct stationery, determine the recipient's correct address, and so on. The point is that a 3-minute egg is not necessarily a 3-minute breakfast.

It is also important to take note of the order of the cycle of activity. There may be three parts to the time something takes, and part 3 may require that parts 1 and 2 be complete. However, it may not matter whether 1 is done before 2 or vice versa. In the case of typing a letter, it makes no difference whether you type the letter or the envelope first. However, it does make a difference in typing the letter whether or not you have determined the recipient's address; if you were to type the letter first you would have to leave room to insert the address.

Timings aid in determining how long it will take to bring the computer system up to speed. You or your secretary may be happy to hand over the filing to the computer, but for the computer to operate, it must have access to the files. That means that you, or someone, will have to enter the files into the computer. In other words, if you are going to have a list of customers that you send letters to each month, each customer's name and address has to be entered into the computer file. If it takes 30 seconds to manually type a new customer's name and address to the existing list, then to enter an existing list of 10,000 names will take 300,000 seconds, of $83\frac{1}{3}$ hours.

ORGANIZING THE INFORMATION

Computers have to be told everything. They have to be told exactly what to expect and what is expected of them. The jargon word GIGO, which stands for garbage in garbage out, is the justification for having an accurate description of what the business system requires. If, for example, a member of the company asks for some information on a report that is neither put into the system nor created by it, then that request is more than just asking for a new line on the report. Once a system has been running for a few months it is often difficult to remember exactly what is being put into the system and exactly what is being taken out.

Input-Output (I/O) Descriptions: What does the system expect from us, and what do we expect from the system—exactly?

An I/O descriptor sheet (see Figure 1) should be prepared for each input and output record. This sheet should include:

1. The name of the record.

2. Some sentences concerning its purpose. (This should include the number of copies and their destination.)

3. A drawing or sample of the record.

It is important that the example of the record be detailed. The length of lines to be filled in and the type of information, whether it is alphabetical or numerical, must be specified.

Let's take the case of an inventory record. The data field that takes the unique inventory number of an item must be as large as the largest number. If, for example, the company has a five-digit inventory number with a two-position alpha code, seven spaces are needed on the sheet of paper that is the input record. Obvious as that is, it tells us that seven spaces are needed in the computer inventory system and that two of those spaces will be alphabetical information. That means that when you purchase an inventory software system, you specify the

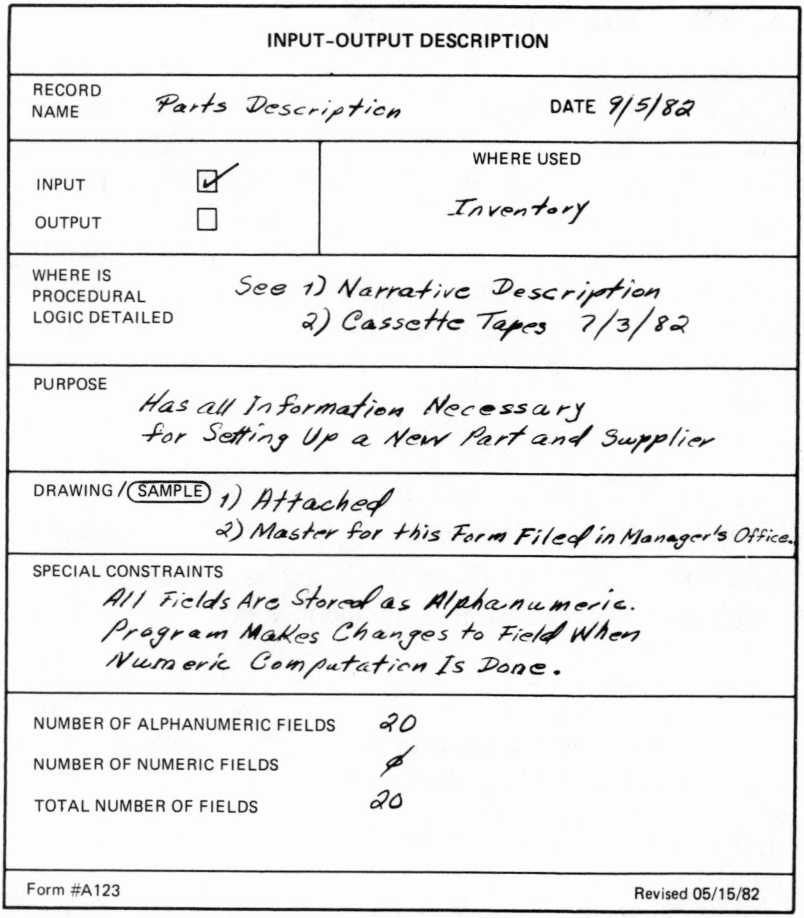

INPUT-OUTPUT DESCRIPTION		
RECORD NAME *Parts Description*		DATE *9/5/82*
INPUT ☑ OUTPUT ☐		WHERE USED *Inventory*
WHERE IS PROCEDURAL LOGIC DETAILED	*See 1) Narrative Description 2) Cassette Tapes 7/3/82*	
PURPOSE	*Has all Information Necessary for Setting Up a New Part and Supplier*	
DRAWING / (SAMPLE)	*1) Attached 2) Master for this Form Filed in Manager's Office.*	
SPECIAL CONSTRAINTS	*All Fields Are Stored as Alphanumeric. Program Makes Changes to Field When Numeric Computation Is Done.*	
NUMBER OF ALPHANUMERIC FIELDS *20* NUMBER OF NUMERIC FIELDS *∅* TOTAL NUMBER OF FIELDS *20*		
Form #A123		Revised 05/15/82

Figure 1

type and length of the fields that will be needed. And the same holds true for any system, from payroll to billing.

Procedure Descriptions: How does it all fit together?

The purpose behind gathering and organizing all the information is to understand the existing system in order to determine the new system. It should not be the purpose of analysis to dictate action for the sake of a new system. Analysis should be used to detail action in order to better understand the system connections and better utilize procedures from a human point of view.

There are three major ways of organizing the information collected in order to highlight the steps of operation. These three are flowcharts, narrative descriptions, and decision tables.

FLOWCHARTS

As the name implies, flowcharts illustrate the movement of work of a particular segment (see Figure 2). Standardized symbols (plastic templates are available at most office or drafting supply companies) are used to get an overall view of the operation. A rectangular box indicates a specific action while a diamond-shaped figure indicates a decision point. Flowcharts are read from top to bottom and highlight the decision points of a system. More detailed charts may add more information to the procedure boxes, but the principle remains the same. A flowchart delineates paths of action and the order of their occurrence.

Flowcharts are built from the lists of information prepared when data was collected earlier. Flowcharts should be cross-referenced to the I/O records.

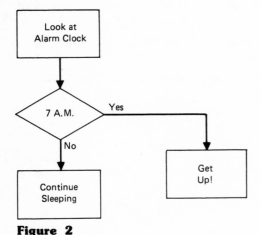

Figure 2

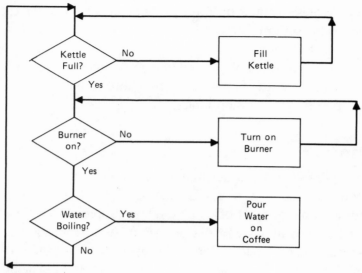

Figure 3

DECISION TABLES

Decision tables are a means of tabulating all criteria involved in a particular decision. Let us look at the example of boiling water to make coffee. A flowchart of the action might be as shown in Figure 3. A decision table would show the same sequence of events, as shown in Figure 4. The value of a decision table is in its inclusion of all pertinent decisions in short form. This means that it can easily be checked with the concerned individuals as to whether or not all decision points have

Is kettle full?	No	Yes	
Is burner on?		No	Yes
Is water boiling?			Yes
Fill kettle	X		
Turn on burner		X	
Pour water on coffee			X

Figure 4

been included. (See Chapter 5 for a more detailed explanation of decision tables.)

NARRATIVE DESCRIPTIONS

A *narrative description* is the written outline of operation procedures. Like the flowchart, it moves in operational sequence—first this is done, then that is done. A narrative description gives you more room to maneuver. In a sense it is a running commentary on the work action.

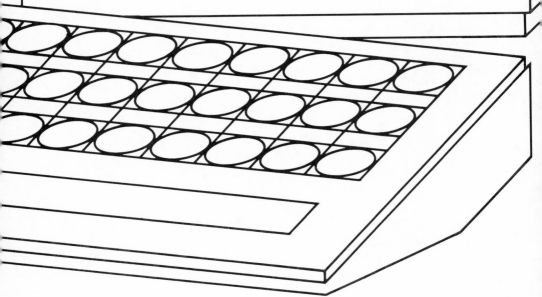

3 THE COM-PUTER AS A TOOL

3 THE COMPUTER AS A TOOL

Computer hardware and software are interdependent. Every computer has input, output, and processor hardware. It also has an operating system and language software. Software choices should always determine hardware choices.

I. HARDWARE AND SOFTWARE—YOU CAN'T HAVE ONE WITHOUT THE OTHER

II. HARDWARE
1. Bits and Pieces: What devices do we need to make up a working computer?
2. Input Devices: How do we get the information into the computer?
3. Output Devices: What do we want to look at after the computer has done its work?
4. Processing Unit: How powerful a computer is needed?

5. Connector Devices: Can we plug the pieces we want into each other?
6. Storage: How does the computer remember everything?

III. SOFTWARE

1. Programming: How much software does the user want to write?
2. Software Concepts: What areas need programs?
3. Compatibility: If necessary, can different programs exchange information?

HARDWARE AND SOFTWARE—YOU CAN'T HAVE ONE WITHOUT THE OTHER

Computers are the power tools of the business world. The difference between an accounting system done by hand and one done by computer is the difference between building a house with hand tools and building one with power tools. The gain in speed and mass production is weighed against attention to detail and individual flexibility. Knowing what the tools do helps you choose the right one for the job (see Figure 5).

HARDWARE

The computer, like any tool, has a handle for the user and an apparatus for performing the operation. Systems analysis views the software as the handle and the hardware as the apparatus. In order to understand the relationship of hardware and software, it is easier to start with a discussion of hardware. However, when it comes to determining what a person needs in a computer system, it is better to find out what software will meet the requirements and then go out to find the hardware. The Software section of Chapter 4 discusses programs that will make a small computer work for the business.

Bits and Pieces: What devices do we need to make up a working computer?

Computer hardware may be divided into the following categories:

1. Input and output devices

2. Processing devices

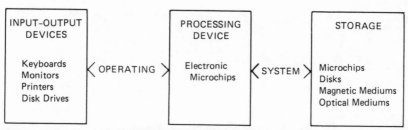

Figure 5 Small Computer Configuration. Shows some of the important technological choices available in these three categories.

3. Storage devices

4. Connectors

A typical, minimal (small) computer configuration, regardless of the size of the computer, has these four attributes. Let's look at the example of a hand-held computer: the input device is the *keyboard*, which allows you to enter information, and the output device is the *display*, which communicates visually to the user in numbers or letters. The processing device is the microchip inside, which is referred to as the *central processing unit* (CPU), or *microprocessing unit* (MPU). The third piece of our hand-held computer storage is another chip that will store this information.

The fourth and final part of any computer are the *connectors*, the things that enable the different parts to plug into each other. And, like everything else, connectors have to be compatible if they are going to get along. Plugs must match physically if they are to be any good. It is necessary to know what kind of connectors a particular piece of hardware uses or expects.

Hardware and software are put together (*configured*) in particular ways for different reasons; but the underlying object is to manipulate information toward a particular end.

In the computer world, the word for the element of stored information is byte. The number of bytes determines the number of characters you can store. Usually this figure is in the thousands. A device that can store around 1000 characters is referred to as having a size or storage capaicty of 1K (1 kilobyte, abbreviated 1 kbyte). A computer storage device of 10,000 bytes is referred to as having 10K memory or capacity. *Memory* usually refers to the CPU, which can be made up of multiple microprocessing units. *Capacity*, on the other hand, is used when talking about data storage media, one step removed from the internal, central processing part of the computer.

Bytes (pronounced bites) are different from bits (pronounced "it" with a "b"). A number of bits make up a single byte. The term *byte* is used to mean a specific unit of information stored by the hardware that can be addressed by the computer.

The following hardware could be put together to form a basic computer:

1. Input devices
   a. Keyboards
   b. Disk drives—need connector device

2. Output devices
   a. Screens
      (1) Cathode ray tubes (CRTs)—known as *monitors*
      (2) Televisions—need connector device
   b. Printers—need connector device
   c. Disk drives—need connector device
   d. Hard disks

3. Processing unit—the microprocessor

4. Connector devices
   a. Interface cards
   b. Buses
   c. Plugs
   d. Modulating devices

5. Storage devices
   a. Disks
   b. Tapes
   c. Magnetic media
   d. Microchips

These are the minimal pieces of equipment that must be looked at. Chapter 4 discusses additional hardware and software that is currently available but, regardless of its type or future development, the above five categories will be of concern for some time. Notice that some devices can act in different capacities. Disks, for example, can be seen as storage devices, input devices, and output devices.

Input Devices: How do we get information into the computer?

These are the pieces of equipment needed to feed information into the machinery.

KEYBOARDS

Keyboard designs fall into two major categories: typewriter and touchkey. However, the important consideration with any keyboard is, "what does it feel like to use?" You don't buy a typewriter without sitting down and getting the feel of it; the same is true of the data entry device of your computer.

Advantages and disadvantages of typewriter keyboards The advantages of the standard typewriter-size keyboard laid out like an office typewriter are that it is easy to use, particularly when you are entering a great deal of information, and it requires little, if any, time to learn. The disadvantage is that its size means you cannot put it in your briefcase or pocket.

Advantages and disadvantages of touchkey keyboards Touchkey keyboards are smaller and the keys may be laid out alphanumerically rather than in the pattern of the standard office typewriter. The major advantage of these devices is their personal portability. Their disadvantage is that they are not efficient in terms of fast data entry over an extended period of time.

DISK DRIVES

Disk drives (or "disks") are an inexpensive means of storing large amounts of information that can be retrieved fairly quickly. Disks come in various sizes. Some standard types are $5\frac{1}{4}$-inch floppy disks, 8-inch floppy disks, and the so-called hard disks.

From the point of view of input, floppy disks can be transferred from one hardware installation to another. That is, you can take a floppy disk that you created in Chicago, mail it to Los Angeles, insert it in the correct size disk drive on a similarly configured hardware/software system, and use it right away. A hard disk, on the other hand, is used for online input, output, and storage. It is not designed for travel.

Floppy disks, because of their portability, are used for entering new software quickly and efficiently. If you purchase word processing software, for example, chances are you will receive a floppy disk that you will read into your setup and utilize.

Output Devices: What do we want to look at after the computer has done its work?

Output devices allow us to see and/or store the results of the computer's work.

SCREENS

Visual display devices that respond instantaneously to computer or operator are known as *screens*.

A video display terminal, often called a VDT, allows the user to see what the computer is saying. Currently, the majority of VDTs are based on cathode ray tubes. CRTs fall into two types: televisions and monitors. The normal home television, whether color or black and white, uses a CRT to form its picture. Utilizing the appropriate connector device, it can be used with a computer as a CRT.

A monitor differs from a television set in that the picture resolution is better. In fact, the video output of a computer is designed to work with monitors. Keep in mind that some software may require a monitor rather than a TV. Monitors come in two screen versions besides color: black-and-white and green screens. Black-and-white screens are less expensive but are a little bit more difficult to view over a prolonged period of time.

PRINTERS

These devices give the user what is known as *hard copy*. The VDT allows you to view information in different aspects, but it can be hard to remember all that is presented. Hard copy, printed information, can be perused at leisure. Also, information may be desired by someone other than the person who has access to the machine, and, lastly, printed material may be needed in the form of invoicing, letters, management reports, and backup master copies.

There are a number of variables to keep in mind when considering a printer. These are:

1. Types of printers.
   a. Dot matrix (letters are formed by small dots). Fast and inexpensive. Ability to change the matrix under software control and so print graphics.
   b. Letter quality (fully formed). Higher print quality, but slower and comparatively more expensive.
   c. Other technologies.

2. Speed of print. The average letter-quality printer has a speed of about 30 lines per minute. The average dot-matrix printer has a speed of about 45 lines per minute. In other words, a report that takes 30 minutes to print with a dot-matrix printer will take 45 minutes with a letter-quality printer.

3. Types of paper.
   a. Fanfolded, tractor-fed computer paper.
   b. Single-sheet, ordinary stationery, usually for letter quality.
   c. Special (thermographic) paper.

4. Width of the print carriage
   a. 80 columns.
   b. 132 or more. Some business software packages requires this size printer.

5. Extra features. The list here can be extensive. The point is that not all extras are luxuries. Some business software packages, for example, require proportional spacing.

6. Interface cards. Printers require an interface to the computer. Sometimes it is built in to either the computer or the processing unit. The question to get answered is: "what interface is required: serial, parallel, or other?" (See the section on connector devices below.)

As with all the equipment, see it in operation under your requirements. If you want five-part forms printed in predetermined places, make sure the printer will meet your requirements.

DISK DRIVES

Because disks are used for both input and output, in other words, transaction storage, backup is of paramount importance. (See the section on the backup process in Chapter 7.)

Backup means that you have a master copy of your information in case, for whatever reason, your data base in destroyed. You may be storing all your general ledger information of disks of either type. One day your office is broken into and the villains throw your disks aside and some get crushed underfoot. Inconvenient, but not disastrous, as it is standard operating procedure to keep spare copies of your disks, updated as frequently as needed, in a safe place—some place different than where you keep your working set.

Different means of storing more and more information on the same size disks are continually being developed. For example, some disk drives write on a single side of the disk. Others write twice as much on a single side—the term is *double density*. And some disk drives write on both sides of the disk, in either single or double density.

Disk-writing compatibility is an important consideration. The operating software is integral to how the information is written. It is quite possible that some packaged software can write to double-density or other types of disks and others cannot. This could be important if you decide later to buy other software packages. Also, you may wish to swap disks with other systems in order to transfer information or provide backup facilities.

The same floppy disk that is used as input may be used as output. If you wish to make sure a floppy disk is not used for output, it can be mechanically *write-protected*. Depending on the size of the floppy disk and the drive manufacturer, a square notch in the side of the disk envelope is either covered or uncovered by a piece of special tape. Currently the majority of $5\frac{1}{4}$-inch disks are write-protected; that is, rendered read-only by covering the notch. The reverse is true for 8-

inch disks. A covered notch enables an 8-inch disk to be written to by the system.

Advantages and disadvantages   The advantage of "floppies" are their portability and comparative inexpensiveness. These reasons give you the added advantage of making backup easy—you just keep an extra set of disks. Their major disadvantage, compared to a hard disk, is that the amount of information that can be stored on any one disk is comparatively small.

HARD DISKS

The so-called hard disk operates in a sealed environment and is permanently online to the computer system. Its major advantage is a greater capacity of online storage with faster physical retrieval. It is more expensive and requires that the system have some other pieces of equipment in order to take backup. With a hard disk, your backup solutions are as follows:

1. Copying the information on to floppy disks.

The problem: one hard disk holds at least 65 to 100 times the amount of information as a floppy disk. It would be tedious and time-consuming in the extreme to have to frequently dump the contents of the hard disk onto floppies.

2. Copying the information onto video recording tapes.

The cost: an interface device between the hard disk and a commercial-quality video machine. This is an efficient means of creating a backup.

3. Combining hard disk and removable cartridge.

This has the advantage of providing unlimited expandability in that some large portion of the data base can be stored on removable hard disks called *cartridges*. Cartridges are more expensive than video tape and may be difficult to justify as a form of archival/ backup storage.

4. **Copying the information onto computer tape.**

Specific recording devices exist to record data onto computer magnetic tape. The advantage of this method is that the recording medium, compared to a disk cartridge, is inexpensive. The disadvantage is that there is an initial cost for another piece of equipment.

As with printers, disk drive technology requires an interface card, usually called a *controller*, which must be purchased separately. Usually one control card will run two floppy disk drives. Multiple hard disk drives usually require an additional piece of hardware in addition to the control card.

Processing Unit: How powerful a computer is needed?

The processing unit is the piece of hardware that makes a computer what it is. It is usually called a *chip*. There are a number of different types of chips. The Z80 and the 6502, for example, are two different manufacturers' microprocessor chips.

The Z80 is used in many different computers, and any manufacturer's Z80-based computer can use software written for the particular operating system (see "Software" below) of a Z80 computer. On the other hand, Z80 software will not normally run on a 6502 computer, although additional hardware is available that can make the 6502 operate with Z80 software with some modification.

Microchips and therefore computers are usually designed to be members of families. That is, the company that makes the Z80, in developing a later microchip, will try to ensure that material that worked on the Z80 will work on the Z8080. Within the family, there is good chance that material will be compatible but always ask. And ask again.

Choosing between different microchips is difficult. At the hardware level, one chip may be faster than another, but from a systems point of view, it is the overall speed of data put through that is of interest. An extreme example might be a new machine with very fast internal cycle time compared to an older, slower computer. However, there may be a great many software packages in existence for the old machine, while a limited amount of software may be available for the new, fast machine.

Also, speed is relative to need. Sometimes a business might not benefit from getting a report instantly as opposed to 48 hours later. (See Chapter 5 for a discussion of designing batch and online systems.)

The point to keep in mind is that the microchip determines the operating system which determines the programming and application packages that are available. Imagine a tree: the microchip is the root, the operating system is the trunk, the programming languages are the branches, and the application packages are the leaves. A tree is not just its roots, not just its leaves—it is everything connected and working together. The same holds true for a computer system.

Connector Devices: Can we plug
the pieces we want into each other.

Very few manufacturers make all the parts for a computer. In fact, the very modularity of a computer is part of its strength. The ability to start with a simple system and add on devices as needs dictate is very cost-effective. A machine that can grow as the business grows and as computer technology changes remains an effective tool over a greater period of time than a machine that is static. It is similar to the music world of turntables, amplifiers, and speakers. It is not always practical to replace the entire system. And it is not always a question of finance. An amplifier that only accepts a cassette player is useless to the person whose music collection is on records.

Although the idea of the compatibility of equipment may appear to be obvious, remember that different manufacturers have different solutions to different problems. In the world of music, cartridge players do not accept cassettes. In the world of video, Betamax tapes cannot be played on VHS machines, and not all video disks can be played on all systems.

Compatibility, what connects to what, must be a major concern of the computer user. With respect to hardware, the two major categories are (1) interface cards and (2) the type of bus.

INTERFACE CARDS

These are boards with electronic circuits that control the communication between the computer and the I/O. A microchip that can function in nanoseconds can obviously produce more information than a device that works in thousandths of a second. Therefore, the flow of information must be regulated.

The computer may be ready to print, but the printer might still be busy with the last line of information. So, the interface card asks the printer if it's ready, the printer says no, and the interface card says to the computer, wait. When the printer is ready and receives the information, the interface checks that it received the information in a form it can use. If the information is acceptable to the printer, then the interface card and the printer shake on the deal. The term "handshaking" refers to the acceptable exchange of information between different devices.

The interface cards for disk drives are known as controllers, while those for printers are known as interface cards. Interface cards for printers are usually only for printers and interface cards for disk drives are usually just for disk drives. However, it is possible to mix and match hardware as computer designs change. Keep in mind that the area to ask questions about is the medium of exchange between the computer and peripheral devices.

Generally, information can be physically moved in two ways, serially or in parallel. Imagine a group of people who want to cross a river. They have two ways of approaching the problem. One school of thought would look for solutions that would transport the group individually, one unit at a time. This is a serial solution to the problem.

The other school would consider solutions that would transport the whole group at once. Here, the units move together, side by side, or in parallel.

Computers hook to peripherals through *ports*, and the number of ports is the limiting size on the number of peripheral devices you can attach at any one time. Again, serial ports accept serial information, parallel ports are for parallel information.

THE BUS

This is a physical configuration which defines electrical pathways between the microprocessor and its peripheral devices. Hardware devices and their connectors must use part or all of this electrical path configuration if they are to attach to each other. Because a particular device may use only part of the configuration, the use of a particular bus structure does not guarantee compatibility. A common standard is the S100 bus.

Regardless of anything else, if you can't plug it in, you can't use it. Just as telephone jacks won't plug into wall sockets, so a certain type of bus accepts only certain types of connectors. Families of computers exist based on the type of bus used.

Storage: How does the computer remember everything?

Regardless of the technology, storage from the point of view of systems analysis (the business system) may be divided initially into two types. The first is what is known as read-write storage, the second is read-only.

READ-WRITE STORAGE

This means that the computer has the ability to read information, manipulate the information in some fashion, and write the information in its new format. the advantage is flexibility, the disadvantage is the accidental change of stored information.

READ-ONLY STORAGE

Information can be read from this medium and acted upon, but information cannot be written to this area. Whatever is in read-only storage is a constant. Read-only storage can be changed, but that usually requires physical intervention.

Advantages and disadvantages The advantages are that information necessary to the operation of the computer system may be stored without fear of accidental change by the operation of the machine. Certain read-only devices are physically separate from the computer storage available to the user and are additional to this storage. Therefore, storage that is available to the user is not used up. Also, with some read-only devices, speed of operation is substantially increased. The only disadvantage of read-only storage is the loss of the option to change data.

Technologically, the types of storage media are disks, tapes, memory media, and microprocessor chips ("microchips").

DISKS

As a storage medium, disks can be read-write or read-only. Magnetic disks can be program-controlled to be read-only or they can be mechanically controlled by the covering or uncovering of a notch. Video disks are currently read-only devices.

Advantages and disadvantages The advantages of disks are that large amounts of data can be stored in a physically small area and can be retrieved quickly and efficiently. The disadvantages of disks are that they are expensive, though this is subject to technological change; they are confusing, because of the number of incompatible types, and they are mechanically complicated and need maintenance.

TAPE

As a storage material, tape is similar to magnetic disks in that it can be read-write or read-only. Read-only types can be program-controlled or mechanically controlled.

Advantages and disadvantages   The major advantage of tape is that it is inexpensive. The disadvantage is that the retrieval of data is slow.

MEMORY MEDIA

This is a catchall term to handle the rapid developments in technology. Different devices are being developed all the time, ranging from magnetic bubble memory to optical read-write devices.

Advantages and disadvantages   The advantages of memory devices are their reliability, because of a lack of mechanical parts, and their storage capacity. The disadvantages are the cost and the problem of compatibility.

MICROCHIPS

As technology develops, it may be possible to envision chips with storage capacities of multimillions of characters.

Advantages and disadvantages   The advantages of microchips are that they are completely electronic and have virtually no mechanical problems. The disadvantage is the problem of compatibility with existing software.

Regardless of the type of technology the important points to consider with storage are:

1. Capacity

2. Speed

3. Backup methods

4. Transportability

5. Availability

6. Price

7. Software compatibility

SOFTWARE

The word "software" is probably a backformation from the engineering world's term "hardware." *Hardware* is the gadgets and things you can pick up or touch with your hands. With the development of operational steps, instructions that were removable yet could be operated on directly by the machine, a new term was needed to describe the instruction program.

Software applies to those things that cannot be physically touched yet are in themselves complete creations, that is, programs. Hardware needs software to operate. It must be told what to do. Software needs hardware, on the other hand, to give it the opportunity to have an effect.

In order to explore this interdependency, let us look at what makes a book. Hardware is a term that may be applied to the book itself. The paper pages, the binding, the glue, and the thread are the physical, or "hardware," aspects of the book. The words and the particular order in which they are written constitute the software. The recipes of a cookbook are software. The narration of a novel is software. Both books may be physically the same with respect to size, weight, type of print, even number of words that can be or are used—this is hardware. However, the order of the words and the result of those words are different depending on the software.

Programming: How much software does the user want to write?

Taking a close look at the recipe book, we notice that recipes have sections. There is a section of instructions which must be done in a particular order; this is the recipe itself and in the computer world is called a program. The other part associated with a particular recipe is a list of ingredients, what the computer world calls data.

A *program* is simply an ordered number of instructions that, when executed in the proper sequence and given the correct data in the proper order at the right time, yields the desired result. As simple as this definition may sound, it is the key to understanding the way of thinking that determines the world of computers. When things go wrong in the computer world, it is because some part of that definition has not been followed.

Going back to the recipe book, let's take a simple recipe for making a plain omelette. The instructions are short: beat some eggs, pour the result into a heated, buttered frying pan, and serve when ready. The ingredients are butter and eggs, and that's it. It doesn't seem as though there is much that could go wrong. However, there are some assumptions built into this recipe.

It is assumed that the person doing the cooking understands the language in which the recipe is written. What about the possibility that the person may be new to the country and just learning the language?

It is assumed that the person knows certain common things. It is conventional, i.e., "everybody knows," that the recipe is done in order, unless otherwise specified. Consider this: the person may be cooking for the first time and may heat the pan before preparing the eggs, and thus end up with an overheated pan.

It is assumed that certain things do not have to be spelled out. The phrase "beat some eggs" means get some fresh eggs, break them gently so that the insides fall into a bowl, and discard the shells. Then, using a fork as an egg beater, whip the yolks and the white together. Consider this alternative: the person doing the cooking may be doing this for the first time—for example, a child.

It is assumed that people know what to do next. There are other instructions that come into use when the omelette is ready. They are such programs of behavior as serving the omelette as a dish at a table, using cutlery rather than fingers to eat the omelette, and cleaning up the dishes and other utensils when finished.

Preparing an omelette and eating it is taken for granted only because we know the steps so well. With computer systems, nothing can be taken for granted. From the above example, the steps are not simply just the few statements of the recipe. And even with our additional considerations, we have not considered the object of the recipe program. In a first explanation of these steps, the recipe would want to make clear that it is necessary to check the eggs. Are the eggs fresh or not? Is the data good or bad? In other words, does the age of the eggs fall within the reasonable boundaries of use?

Reasonableness is a term used to determine the acceptable limits of correct data. Error checking, on the other hand, is used to determine whether or not the correct data item is being utilized. It would be an error, for example, if the recipe calls for an egg and the cook reaches for an orange.

The point of all this is to bring home the fact that computers are best viewed as idiot savants. A computer, the hardware and the software, will only do what it is told. Everything has to be spelled out, and it must be said in a way that the computer understands.

The problem with computers is not that they are complicated, but rather that they are very simple. Everything has to be explained. Assume nothing. There is an old saying in the business world that is taught to all salespeople by their managers. Whenever you *assume* something, it means you make an *"ass* of *u* and *me."* The same is true with computers. The only difference is that the computer doesn't care if it makes an ass of itself.

Software Concepts: What areas need programs?

The purpose of a computer system is to do boring, repetitive functions without getting bored or tired. To achieve this, a system is set up, using whatever tools are needed. Hardware, software, and whatever else is necessary are used as tools within the system.

Every business utilizes an accounting system. To do accounting, the business does certain things on a timely basis in order to keep track of its finances. There are certain steps that have to be followed in order to prepare invoices. These steps are the program that must be followed. Many small businesses use manual accounting systems where the instructions, the programs, are printed in a book. This book, along with rules for utilizing it, are bought as a package.

Similar packages are available for computers. Programs are usually stored on disks and the instructions are usually printed in an accompanying manual. The term for these packets of information is *packages.* Buying a package saves time since it eliminates the need for writing a program from scratch and having to document the program and how to use it. Different types of packages are designed to do different things, and not all packages interface with each other.

A data base management package may have a list of the names and addresses of all your clients. You may want to send a letter to your customers announcing a new service or a change in policy. However, the data base management package is not able to generate form letters. The generation of form letters requires a word processing package of some type, and it may not be able to use the names and addresses stored by the data base management package. All the names and addresses may have to be entered by hand, or a special program may have to be written to do the conversion.

Never assume that because the data is stored on a disk by one program it can be used by another program in another package.

The computer world is organized around two principles: hierarchy and synergy. *Hierarchy* is an ordered series of things. *Synergy* is the process of discrete things working together to achieve an effect greater than the sum of the parts.

Computers speak in codes, and so a collection of codes that talk directly to the machine is logically enough called *machine language* (see Figure 6). Machines find it extremely easy to understand codes written in machine language. Unfortunately, people find it difficult and slow.

Machine languages are known as *low-level languages* in that this is the lowest level one can use in communicating with the machine. Machine languages are fast in operation and take up little room in memory. On the other hand, they are difficult to understand and slow to write. This means a high cost must be paid for trained personnel.

To make life easier for people, languages that are easier to understand have been developed. Common codes are referred to by human language characters rather than machine language characters, one uses alphabetic codes instead of numeric codes. Because these codes are a step further away from the machine, they are known as *high-level languages*.

BASIC, COBOL, Pascal, FORTRAN, FORTH, and numerous others are high-level languages. Because they are easier for humans to write and understand, personnel costs are lower. On the other hand, they are slower in operation and take up more memory. Different high-level languages exist for a number of reasons, including historical precedence in development and type of job application. At the present

Level	Name	Requirement	Considerations
Higher	Program generators	Intermediary Software	Good for standard applications. User must do all the analysis. Not very flexible.
	Data base query language		Fairly flexible if you need to change the data base. Requires detailed knowledge of package to use well.
High	BASIC COBOL Pascal		Difficult to change data base. Requires detailed knowledge of package to use well.
	Assembler		Very difficult to use. Efficient use of machine.
Low	Machine language	None	Extremely difficult. Very efficient use of machine.

Figure 6   Language Chart. Note that the lower the level the older the language.

time, BASIC and Pascal are the two main high-level languages in use with small computers. Ada is expected to become a standard language because of its acceptance by the U.S. government, however, This would follow the pattern of COBOL, which was accepted by the U.S. government in the late 1960s and became the standard for the 1970s.

Regardless of the language, keep in mind that languages are sold as packages by different manufacturers. Therefore Radio Shack's BASIC is not exactly the same as Apple's BASIC. Also, a single language may have different versions, and an application program may be written for one version and not operate on another. Computer games for the Apple, for example, require integer BASIC, while application programs use floating-point BASIC. Computers, therefore, may speak different dialects of the same language.

In general, high-level languages are considered somewhat inefficient in that one command has to generate a great deal of generalized code. One COBOL command, for example, could generate up to 40 machine commands. However, not all high-level languages are necessarily inefficient in operation. By matching a language to the specific architecture of a machine or family of machines, the language generates only the needed commands. The language remains portable within the family, is easier to use than machine language, and is fairly efficient in compilation. In other words, the ratio of translation of system language commands to machine language commands is quite small.

The mechanisms that translate a high-level language into a machine code are known as compilers and interpreters. An *interpreter* sits inside the computers and operates at the same time as the high-level language program. A *compiler*, on the other hand, takes the high-level program and creates or compiles a program in machine code, which is then entered into the computer.

Interpreted programs are slow and take up space, but they are easy to modify. Compiled programs are faster and occupy less space, but are harder to modify during use.

Compatibility: If necessary, can different programs exchange information?

Languages are ultimately a collection of commands. When commands are put together in such a way so as to perform a specific function, they are seen as a *routine*. And a collection of routines that is complete in itself is seen as a program. There are two major types of programs: application programs and operating system programs.

Application programs allow the user to apply the power of the computer to a particular job. These programs may be specific to the job, such as an accounts payable program, or to types of jobs, such as updating files or producing reports. A data base management package, for example, may allow you to tailor it in such a way that it keeps track of your receivables and prints invoices.

Programs that have this much user flexibility are almost high-level languages in themselves. Many application programs and operating system programs fall into this category of languagelike utility.

The original idea of operating system programs was to organize and run the computer so that the hardware and software could operate as a single, efficient system. This meant that every device attached to the computer had to be able to perform its function without disrupting other devices and hopefully without tying up processing time.

Because hardware was until recently too expensive to dedicate to a single task, software solutions, operating systems, were developed. With the advent of inexpensive memory, it is now practical to build machines with built-in I/O routines that are part of the overall computer system. Software operating systems remain of concern to the user in two aspects: disk operating systems and multiuser environments.

Disk operating systems take care of the physical placement of the bytes of information of the disk. When a program running in the computer needs a specific piece of information, it is the disk operating system that acts as the traffic cop. It is the disk operating system, not the program, that knows where to go for the information that the program needs. Therefore, it is important that the program, the disk operating system, and the disk all be compatible. Problems occur when information is written, placed on the disk by one disk operating system, and then an attempt is made to read it by another. This situation can arise when different versions, releases of the same disk operating system, are used. Version 1, released at the beginning of the year, might lay out information on the disk according to one scheme. Later in the year, a new release of the disk operating system may lay out information differently. And so disks from version 1 will have to be upgraded for version 2.

Disk operating systems are often written into software packages. For example, a word processing package may write to disks according to its own disk operating system. Therefore, an accounting package may not be able to read information from those disks.

Compatibility of operating systems is an important consideration with some computer families because they may designate everything outside of the main processing unit as a user. So the printer, the disk drives, and so on are seen as users. The operating system then acts as a traffic cop to the whole computer. The next step up is to link numerous processing units together. Again, the operating system is the traffic cop of the situation.

The systems analyst's concern with the details of operating systems software is its applicability to the business system. The higher the level of interaction between different parts of the business system, the more compatibility is required of different operating systems software. If a computer system is to be used for only one thing at a time, for example word processing and accounts receivable, and information in one system is not required by the other, then system compatibility may be low on the list of priorities. If the requirement is that the word processor system use information from the accounts receivable system under program control, then operating system compatibility is a high priority.

Choosing a system is always a trade-off between budget and available options. Software is no exception. Software is the language of computers. For a language to work, whether it is called English, Chinese, COBOL, or disk operating system, it must satisfy three requirements. It must have description elements, conditional elements, and active elements. A language has to answer what, how, and when.

The fastest software is written directly for the machine. The slowest is written for human beings. A sort routine written in machine code is not understandable to the general public and is of little help to the secretary who wishes to sort the list of customer checks received that month. A sort routine that is geared to the secretary and asks for the name and the order of sorting in English-like words is much easier to use—for people. And a sort routine that doesn't even bother to ask because it's part of a specific accounts receivable system is the easiest of all.

What you gain in ease, you lose in flexibility. But often a business doesn't want flexibility at a detailed level. Rather, it wants the job done by a system that is easy to operate.

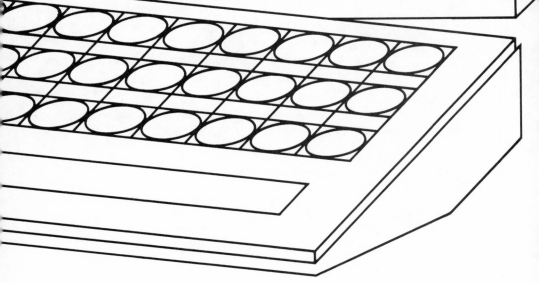

4 OPENING UP YOUR SYSTEM

4 OPENING UP YOUR SYSTEM

Determine what equipment can be utilized by your system. Provide guidelines for choosing specific hardware and software.

I. WHAT ENABLES YOU TO DO WHAT

II. HARDWARE
1. Card Readers: Do I have to keep track of items used by different people?
2. Touch-Sensitive Devices: Do I need easy, unambiguous data entry?
3. Digitizers: Do I need a lot of graphic input?
4. Voice Recognition: Are the system user's hands available?
5. Optical Character Readers: Do I have a lot of text input?
6. Plotters: Do I need line-quality graphics?
7. Typewriter Interfaces: Do I have small letter-quality printing needs.
8. Vocal Output: Do I need to hear what is going on?
9. Memory Typewriter: Do I need some formatting of my letter-quality printing?
10. Copiers: How can I back up my printer?
11. Microfilm/Microfiche: Is hard copy storage space a problem?
12. Networks and Telephone Lines: Do I need to have my computer talk to other systems?

III. SOFTWARE

1. Word processing: Do I need to manipulate words and the printed result?
2. Mailing Programs: Do I need varied mailings of letters to preprocessed addresses?
3. Electronic Spread Sheets: Do I need to simulate a situation and ask "what if?"
4. Electronic Filing Systems: Am I interested in sorting and selecting records?
5. Data Base Management Systems: Do I need to sort, select, and process my information in ways I cannot yet envision?
6. Business Packages: Can I buy an existing program or set of programs that will meet most of my needs?
7. System Utilities: Do I need to get involved with the nuts and bolts of the system?
8. Programming Aids: Do I need custom software, and what is available to make it easier to produce?
9. Communication Packages: What do I need to enable my system to talk to other systems?

WHAT ENABLES YOU TO DO WHAT

If you think of a computer as an electronic brain, you might consider the system to be the body in which it resides. In the human body, the eyes accept visual input, the ears accept auditory input, the nose accepts olfactory input, the tongue determines taste, the body utilizes the mouth for audible output, and the hands determine touch and are used for graphic output.

Now, let's look at a small computer system. Visual input might appear to be difficult, but there are a number of peripheral devices that operate on this principle. Video cameras, for one, feed pictures to the CPU, and the computer can then enhance the picture. Computers that hear on a limited basis are already available, but what about a computer that can smell? Chemical laboratories attach numerous devices to small computers to perform that very function.

Peripheral devices feed information to the CPU so that it can process, organize, and select all the data. The human brain performs these functions by following certain rules of manipulation and protocol. With computers, it is software that provides the CPU with the rules and protocol.

Extending the analogy further, the human body does not exist in isolation. The same should be true of a business system that uses a small computer. Not every tool has to be attached to the machine to be considered a part of the system. Your office typewriters are part of your information flow. The copying machine is an integral part of your business system and should be used in conjunction with the computer.

Because computers seemingly do everything, we sometimes forget that they do not have to do it all. Often cost is a reason, sometimes time, but the point is that a small computer business system should take advantage of the many existing peripheral devices and software packages available.

HARDWARE

In the world of computer talk, everything that is not the CPU but is connected to it is *peripheral equipment*. The keyboard, the printer, and the disk drives are all peripheral devices. In addition, there are, from the overall systems view, unconnected devices that can be utilized with a small computer in order to inhance the flow of information. All devices, whether peripheral or unconnected, fall into the general categories of input and output.

INPUT DEVICES

There are a number of ways of getting information into your system. The keyboard is perhaps the most familiar, but other devices do exist.

Card Readers: Do I have to keep track of items used by different people?

This device usually accepts IBM-style cards. They are worth considering as data collection devices. At the point of activity, you might use cards to keep track of printed material in a library or an inventory check-out situation.

Touch Sensitive Devices: Do I need easy, unambiguous data entry?

There are two varieties. The first is set up to make the screen of your VDT sensitive to touch. This is convenient if people don't want to use the keyboard or if you want to force a simple choice. Basically, it enables the user to just touch what they want on the screen.

Another variation is the touch pad, which is used in a peripheral device that can read your handwriting. Your paper form is fitted on the touch-sensitive pad, and as you print, the characters are fed directly to the CPU. This type of device can eliminate intermediary data entry steps. It might be used in telephone ordering, where the operator takes down the basic information on the form, and it is then fed directly to the system.

Advantages   The advantages of this type of device over something like a portable keyboard are twofold. Many people prefer writing to typing, and a hard copy in the person's handwriting is generated immediately.

Digitizers: Do I need a lot of graphic input?

This is what you use when you want to draw something for your machine. You move the pointer along the line on the paper, and it is converted into x, y coordinates that can be displayed on the screen and stored away.

Entering graphs, map outlines, and schematics is much easier with this type of device. You can take any picture and define its two-dimensional outline by a collection of x, y coordinates. One way is to figure them out by hand and feed them via the keyboard. The digitizer makes life much easier.

Use a digitizer to enter preprinted graphic information, and then use your computer not only to analyze the shape information but also to graphically manipulate it. A business application for this type of device might be in a real estate development office, where existing land maps and development plans can be entered into storage.

A note of caution: Graphics manipulation with small computers is possible, but at the moment it requires some expertise on the part of the user.

Voice Recognition: Are the system user's hands available?

Now you can talk to your computer—within limits. Computers have a limited recognition vocabulary and require some preciseness of diction on the part of the user. This type of device is perfect when the user's hands are already occupied. Checking parts on an assembly line or dispensing prescriptions in a pharmacy are tasks which lend themselves to voice recognition. Something to keep in mind is that to take full advantage of voice recognition some programming, if not a great deal of it, may be required.

Optical Character Readers: Do I have a lot of text input?

Optical character readers have been around for some time. They look like copy machines and are operated in a similar manner. A sheet of paper with printed text is placed face down on the reading screen and the machine converts the text into electronic information. The text must be in some standard typeface.

It is not usually economically feasible to have an optical character reader online to a small business system. What is sensible is to consider using a commercial word processing office to read in the information and store it on a disk medium that is readable by your computer.

There are a number ot things to keep in mind if you are looking to store a great deal of existing printed material on your computer system:

1. Do you really need to?

2. What typeface will the optical character reader read?

3. What electronic character code format will the result take?

4. What physical format will the storage take?

Utilization of this type of outside peripheral device requires that you check, test, and check again before committing yourself.

A use for this type of device would be in a situation where many district offices are set up with their own small computers. If a great deal of typed material has to be looked at and processed by a number of people, it is worth considering this machine. Publishing houses, for example, receive numerous typed sheets that are processed by many different people from editors to illustrators, while large corporations often produce extensive reports from existing material.

Advantages and disadvantages   The advantage of this type of machine is the increased speed of entry over that of having to retype hundreds of pages into a computer. However, the disadvantage is that these devices are extremely expensive. Usually, large corporations and certain large word processing businesses own them.

OUTPUT DEVICES

Plotters: Do I need line-quality graphics?

In a sense, these are the reverse of digitizers. What these machines do is draw the pictures your computer generates. Plotters draw smooth, continuous lines compared to printers, which create the illusion of a line by overlapping dots. Plotters use pens of either a special type or a commercially available type found in art and drafting stores. This means that even with a single-pen plotter you could change the colors on your output. Multiple-pen plotters are not that uncommon and are quite affordable. Plotters are to graphic output what letter-quality printers are to text output.

Advantages   The advantage of this type of device is in the preparation of line drawings, diagrams, and schematics. A plotter is very helpful if you use charts in presentations or have a use for line illustration.

Typewriter Interfaces: Do I have small
letter-quality printing needs?

It is possible to connect your existing typewriter to your computer and have it act as a printer. There are two approaches to doing this.

In one, mechanical plungers are positioned over the keys, and the computer uses them to type out its material. Because these interfaces are mechanical, they can easily slip out of adjustment and require a fair bit of fiddling. The other approach is an electronic interface to certain specific electric or electronic typewriters. Set them up once and you can forget about the interface.

Interface devices are best used as subsidiary machines. An inexpensive dot-matrix printer could do the bulk of your printing, and the 30 to 40 times a month that you require letter quality, you could use your interfaced typewriter. Salespeople or others who take small computers on the road might use them for generating four to five letters or short reports when they are in a strange office.

Advantages   The advantage of these types of interface is that for a fraction of the cost of a letter-quality printer you have letter-quality printing.

Disadvantages   The disadvantages are numerous. You do not have all the special features of a letter-quality printer available to you, such as proportional spacing, multiple single-sheet feeding, conversion to tractor feeding when required, and the ability of the printer to respond to program control. There is an additional serious drawback. Typewriters are designed to be used by people. Mechanically, they are not set up to take the sort of continuous output that a computer generates. It's not the expense of the additional service calls your typewriter will require, which it will, that is an issue; it is the expense of *down time*, the time that the equipment is not available for your use, that is important.

Vocal Output: Do I need to hear what is going on?

Inexpensive devices which make small computers talk are available. A number of methods exist for doing this, and the size of the vocabulary is not a problem. There is, for example, a product that will say any message that your programs print on the screen. One thing to look for is the quality of sound. You need a voice that is not irritating and that can be distinctly heard and understood.

Advantages   The primary advantage of this type of peripheral device is that it frees the operator from having to be in constant attendance. Small computers are often occupied with internal processing for 10 to 15 minutes at a time. The psychological advantage of being able to leave the machine alone and do something else without staring at the screen is immense.

Vocal output tends to make the machine softer and more approachable. People anthropomorphize machines anyway. A machine that answers back lends the computer to being used in any type of learning situation.

Disadvantages   Perhaps the disadvantages of a vocalizing computer is that people will begin to expect too much of it. But this is a doubtful objection, at best.

Memory Typewriters: Do I need some
formatting of my letter-quality printing?

These are typewriters that allow electronic text correction and layout. The typewriter is upgraded to a responsive mechanism utilized by a human operator; however, it is not connected to the computer. The major problem of all textual output from the point of view of the business user is format. A memory typewriter has the ability to operate on a limited amount of internally stored text.

Advantages   The advantage to a small business is that the computer may be dedicated to information retrieval or accounting, and it may not be available for use as a word processor. If your finished copy needs are not great, 30 or 50 pages a day, then a memory typewriter may be the effective solution.

Disadvantages   The disadvantage of this type of machine is its inability to create multiple, yet slightly different, variations of material automatically. It is not the best answer for a mass mailing.

Copiers: How can I back up my printer?

Electronic copiers can be integrated quite successfully into a small computer system. Copy shops are common and easily accessible. Computer-generated output can be transferred to your own stationery if a plain paper copier is available. Also, it is often cheaper in both time and money to use copiers rather than multiple-part paper or duplicate computer runs. Some computer printers utilize specially coated papers for printing. These papers will fade after approximately 6 months' exposure to light, however, while a copier provides you with permanent archival material.

Microfilm/Microfiche: Is hard copy storage space a problem?

Computers generate an enormous amount of paper. It is not always possible to eliminate it all, and storage can become a problem. In many cities, there are firms that will put your material on microfilm or microfiche. You can always use the computer to index them and provide you with an up-to-date catalogue.

Networks and Telephone Lines: Do I need to have my computer talk to other systems?

All the previous devices allow the systems designer to use computers efficiently within a system. Another way of extending the power of a system relates to the adage "two heads are better than one." With computers, it means that the CPU can talk to other CPUs or other peripheral devices by plugging into a network. Just as we pick up the phone and get information from 3000 miles away, so can the computer.

The jargonists are trying to take over the word "network" and assign it specific meanings in different areas. However, the basic sense of the word remains. A computer network is just like a people network—it's who you know, who you can talk to, that determines the information you can get and the influence you can wield.

Computers often link up locally by cable, and so they know everyone in the building. This is what's meant by a local network. If your business is on three floors and you have one computer on the ground floor and one on the top floor, there are numerous reasons to have them talk to each other. The downstairs computer may want to print something, but there's only one printer, and it's on the third floor. Or the third-floor computer may need some information that the downstairs computer knows.

The next step up from this is giving the computer access to the telephone. An inexpensive device called a *modem* (it stands for modulator-demodulator) is required at each end of the telephone line. Now the extent of the network is limited only by the user group's imagination.

Access by telephone to the business data base means that office workers do not necessarily have to work in the office. After all, word processing on a small computer could be done at home, and the results sent over the wire to be read on the office computer VDT or printed out in hard copy. If more than one employee has access to a terminal or computer at home, they could all communicate and work together without going to work. It's the work that travels, not the worker.

In many cities, there are electronic bulletin boards which allow network subscribers to leave messages for each other, to exchange programs, and to gather and disseminate information. Communications networks are available that provide access to numerous data bases, allow the transmission of printed material (electronic mail), and offer services such as buying theater and airline tickets.

The ability to network requires both hardware and software. It is not enough to just plug your computer into the phone line. Different networks have different rules governing the movement of information. These rules are known as the *protocol* for that network.

Networking can increase the computing power of a small computer enormously by having your machine call up a larger machine. Your system pays for its share of time on the main computer. Basically, your computer acts as the terminal, while the larger computer acts as the CPU.

Anything that can be encoded can be stored and transmitted over wires or through space. This means that the possible sources of input and output for a small computer system are astronomical. With a small computer, you are not limited to the traditional functions of word processing and accounting. The computer can become a research assistant and general, all-around "gofer."

Small computers may be linked to the stock market via telephone. Certain banks offer the choice of banking by computer, and it's possible to utilize teletype facilities using a small computer. The ability of small computers to link into travel agency information could save a business countless hours of working out travel details and ticket bookings.

A computer doesn't just get information, it gets it selectively. It is this attribute that makes it such a powerful tool in networking. A small computer can save you days of researching in the library and reading articles. Large national data bases of articles, bibliographies, and journals are available to be searched by computer.

Networking can be used for computer conferencing. By having a central pool of large files, different executives can work on the same project at the same or different times. The work is always current and instantaneously available.

SOFTWARE

It takes about 50 days of work to solve, write, and document an average application program. Instead of reinventing the wheel, business people often purchase existing software.

Advantages   The major advantages of off-the-shelf software are that it is available now, so that you do not have to spend time creating the tools that make the tools. Off-the-shelf software is inexpensive. Time is money and, as one of hopefully a large base of buyers, you pay only a fraction of the cost. Finally, it usually works, and there is support when it doesn't. That is, you have someone to talk to when things go wrong. Often this means the errors are found and corrected. Sometimes it just means that someone out there understands your problem. They can't do anything about it, but at least they know what you're ranting and raving about. After sitting up all night with a crabby system, a sympathetic ear can be worth the cost of a week in the mountains.

Disadvantages   The major disadvantages of off-the-shelf software are that it won't always do exactly what you want, it will only do 90 percent of it. That 10 percent gap could be crucial. On the other hand, it might work fine, but in 2 years the company that produced it might go bust, and it may begin to act funny. This is rare and becoming more so as the small computer world grows up and establishes standards.

Word Processing: Do I need to manipulate words and the printed result?

Word processors are like food processors: they take the work out of cutting, chopping, and mixing. In simple terms, word processors are made up of two parts: an editor and a formatter.

Basically, the editor allows the author to write and revise the original material. The formatter takes that material and lays it out in its final printed form. Different packages offer different approaches to and capabilities in these two areas.

Choosing the correct word processor for your needs becomes easier when you list your needs. Comparing all the possible functions of different word processing packages is secondary. The first thing to do is determine who will use it and for what reason.

Most writers fall into these four categories:

1. Authors want to be free to create and re-create.

2. Publishers want to be free to have extensive control of the layout.

3. Form writers want quick and easy production of repetitious formatted material.

4. Report writers want footnotes, subscripts, columns of numbers, and everything in between.

THE AUTHOR

An author needs ease of operation. The fewer the key strokes, the better. Long, intense periods of effort will be spent at the machine, and so screen response time must be fast. The best type of program is one that doesn't require any intellectual effort on the part of the user.

THE PUBLISHER

Whether it be a newsletter or a book, the publisher needs a great deal of creative control in layout manipulation. What it all looks like, exactly, on the printed page is of principal importance.

FORM WRITER

Forms can be anything from letters to invoices. They are standardized documents that are customized by filling in the blanks. In this situation, the operator needs something that is easy to learn and easy to use. It does not have to be overly complicated, yet it should provide some degree of formatting control. Because a large number of form letters may be required for individual mailings, easy access to an adequate mailing list program is a consideration.

REPORT WRITER

Reports are usually made up of lots of different material that is then brought together into a single format. Access to data base files and the ability to easily process numeric characters are advantages. The ability to handle large files easily and the ability to do some fairly complex formatting are major considerations.

Mailing Programs: Do I need varied mailings of letters to preprocessed addresses?

These are often separate programs. These packages provide the automatic insertion of customer names and addresses into form letters. In simple terms, what they do is run your edited text against your mailing list. They also provide you with the ability to manipulate your mailing list with sort and select functions.

Electronic Spread Sheets: Do I need to simulate a situation and ask "what if?"

These programs let you lay out a very large sheet of electronic graph paper. Then you divide the sheet into columns and rows. These columns and rows can then be labeled and the entries related according to some formula. They are used extensively in financial planning to ask, "what if?"

Packages like this enable you to build certain mathematical models. A mathematical model uses numbers and relationships to build a model of a situation as a craftsperson uses wood to build a working model of an airplane that a company is thinking of building. The plane model might be designed to try out wings with different lengths to see how they affect the overall performance. Obviously it is easier and cheaper to build a model.

Electronic spread sheets use numbers (instead of wood, as in the example above), for their models. A simple mathematical model is a yearly budget. A complex mathematical model might be used to try to describe the economy. These types of programs take time to learn and use properly, and the more complex the model, the greater the setup time.

Advantages   The advantage of only these packages comes in their ability to make almost instantaneous changes to the data of the model. They are useful to anyone who does financial management, from the individual budget to the corporate bottom line.

Electronic Filing Systems: Am I interested
in sorting and selecting records?

These packages allow you to store data in some format, usually
records, and print them according to certain sort and select criteria.
Built into these packages is the report generator. This gives the user
some control over formatting the data into readable hard copy. The
packages can be quite sophisticated and allow certain limited arithme-
tic operations to be performed within the record and the report. Often
they are mistakenly called data base management systems.

Data Base Management Systems: Do I need to sort, select,
and process my information in ways I cannot yet envision?

Data base management systems do all the things that an electronic
filing system does and more. The "and more" refers to the fact that
some form of query language is available to the user, and that the
words of the language can be stored and used as programs. There are
enormous theoretical differences between file managers and data base
managers. Data base management systems are more complex and
usually faster internally, and they require large amounts of memory.
However, as technology moves forward, these differences are of little
concern to the end user.

In a very narrow sense, the difference between an electronic filing
system and a data base management system is that the first has only a
report generator while the latter has a query language. A data base
management system is more flexible but concomitantly more difficult
to use than an electronic filing system. It's like going out for a fast food
meal or a gourmet dinner: the electronic filing system will satisfy the
basic hunger, but a data base management system improves the
quality of computer life.

Business Packages: Can I buy an existing program
or set of programs that will meet most of my needs?

There are packages available for most of the common business
functions. Accounting, inventory, payroll, and others are standard.
Specific industry applications also exist, such as legal and medical
billing.

Again, the advantage of a package is that you know that it works. The disadvantage is that it might not do what you want in the way you want.

System Utilities: Do I need to get involved with the nuts and bolts of the system?

These are programs that allow you to poke and probe your system. They can be diagnostic aids or tools to help you keep the hardware and software better organized. Most business people should not have to deal with them.

Programming Aids: Do I need custom software, and what is available to make it easier to produce?

A craftsperson never has one tool. There are tools to make tools and tools to make life easier. That's the function of programming aids. The aid you need depends on the language that you use and what you want to use it for. They are of no interest to the businessperson.

Communication Packages: What do I need to enable my system to talk to other systems?

Once you start linking computers together, you need something to organize and keep track of all that talking. There are software packages which help you sign on to national networks, take advantage of automatic dialing hardware, act as a negotiator between big machines and small machines, and everything else in between.

Electronic mail, for example, makes your computer behave as a mailbox. It has to receive the mail, give it only to the person with the right key, and pick up your mail to deliver it to the correct address. A communication package is what makes it act that way.

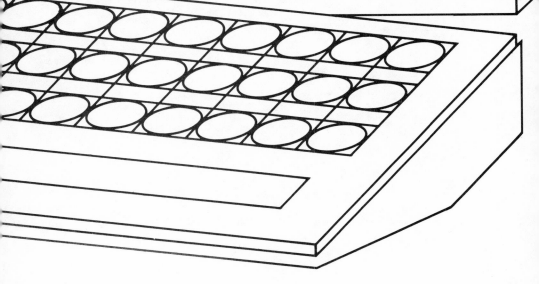

5 DESIGNING A NEW SYSTEM

5 DESIGNING A NEW SYSTEM

Software comes before hardware. Lay out the rules and regulations for how things are done. Specify the process of your business from the viewpoint of the things it does.

I GETTING WHAT YOU WANT

II CHARTING TECHNIQUES

1. Function charts: What has to be done?
2. System Boundaries: How much do I expect a particular area to handle?
3. Work Down: Do I have the details of what goes in, what changes occur, and what comes out?
4. Decision Tables: Have I defined and set out all the logical rules?
5. Flowcharts: Do I know where everything is going?
6. PERT: Have I figured out when things have to happen and how much time they require?

III FORMS ANALYSIS

1. Data Flow: Do the hand and eye move smoothly?
2. Logic: Does the form help to ensure that the right information is put in the right place at the right time?
3. Requirements: Does the form meet the needs of the equipment?

IV SECURITY/PRIVACY

1. Encryption Devices: Have I limited access to the rules of formation?
2. Passwords: Have I limited access to the data?
3. Locks: Have I limited access to the equipment?

GETTING WHAT YOU WANT

Confronted by the myriad choices of the computer industry, even an experienced programmer or computer consultant, let alone a new user, is often overwhelmed. As with any activity, where to begin is often the most difficult step.

In the late 1950s, when business computers were first mass-marketed, the machines were difficult to manipulate. This led to the fostering of an attitude that the user had to adjust his business behavior to the demands of the equipment. Of course, this was never completely true. However, by operating as if this were the case, many businesses fell into the trap of misplaced priorities.

Tools are designed for us to more effectively control our environment. Any tool that makes our task more difficult threatens the continued existence of the task. Any business that loses sight of its main goal and dedicates itself to its operating system is bound to fail. It doesn't matter if the operating system is built around state-of-the-art computers or 10,000 trained clerks. If the reason for the system is ignored, then the system will eventually fail.

An insurance company exists to sell insurance. It is obvious that a computer system that impedes this function is not going to last long. But what about the horror stories? The need for highly trained people who can talk to computers. The computer errors that we all confront in our daily lives. And, worst of all, haven't we all had to do something a particular way because the machines require it?

Let's not confuse compromise with giving in. Also, let's not confuse ends with means. Consider what the proverb is telling us when it talks of missing the forest for the trees.

A tool, any tool, only exists in subservience to the user's purpose. It doesn't matter if the tool is a hammer, a computer, or a 5-year business plan, it is always judged by what use you, the user, can get out of it.

So, when someone in the department complains about the forms that have to be filled out differently because of the new computer system, chances are they are complaining about having to change their routine. From the point of view of the department, the inconvenience of learning a new system is weighed against the convenience of increased human productivity.

Keep in mind that computers have created more jobs than they have eliminated. That does not mean that there are not individual or group cases of hardship. New skills will always replace old, and learning new skills is not always easy.

Small computers will force us to determine and delineate our needs. Instead of turning us into idle morons served by automatons, as the horror writers would have it, we will be forced to think more clearly and make more decisions of increasing human value.

Consider the ultimate computer but one. I don't consider the ultimate computer because, as soon as I do that, there will be something I did not consider and so, it is beyond the ultimate computer. Therefore, it is by definition the ultimate computer.

The point to this aside is the illustration of a systematic way of thinking. I want my use of the example clearly understood. As the user of this example, I determine the definition. That's the user's prerogative and it is the reader's prerogative to accept my definition or not. So, consider the ultimate computer but one.

The businessperson will arrive at the office and address the computer in everyday language. The machine will be called SLV-2-U or SLV for short, and the future businessperson will say:

"Good morning. I'd like all the relevant details on the EXCO deal. Call the club and get me a court for 11:00. Oh yes, I want to increase my take-home profit by 10 percent for this year."

Seemingly nothing could be easier than that. No programmers. No sitting at keyboards, no turning on of equipment. No codes, data elements, files, or records. What could be simpler?

However, how does the businessperson know what statements to make? And how does the machine understand them? In the first instance, the businessperson has to be clear as to what needs to be dealt with, i.e., "the EXCO deal." Why not the YCO deal? Secondly, the businessperson has to ask a reasonable question, i.e., "increase my take-home profit by 10 percent for this year." Why not 5 or 50 or 1000 percent?

And the machine, who explained to it what is meant by relevant? How does SLV know that the businessperson is willing to increase productivity in one area in order to get the extra 10 percent?

Nothing comes from nothing. Everything has its place in a universe that is in dynamic balance. Computers do not perform miracles. They may be able to manipulate many more things many times faster than we can, but the statements and questions still have to be asked.

Small computers will increasingly force us to confront our individual and societal values. After all, having asked the machine how to increase profit by 10 percent we are going to want to know the cost. A legitimate but unreasonable answer might well be, "sell the business—the capital value will increase your profit this year by 10 percent."

Small computers will force us to ask more and more questions and force us to consider their relevancy. Analysis is, of course, the classic tool for determining questions. Systems analysis is the tool for determining their dynamic relevancy. So, having said all this, are we any closer to knowing where to begin?

Analysis would say to start anywhere, just start differentiating. And, in itself, it is a good technique for getting started. But getting started is not always enough. We may start down a blind alley and waste time or follow a path that leads us to the wrong place. Systems analysis would ask, "where do we want to get to and why?"

It is ironic that the soulless, cruel machines of the 1960s and 1970s, the machines that generated freedom and creativity's battle cry of "don't spindle, bend, or mutilate," were the precursors of machines that will force us to be more creative and more aware of our human freedoms. After all, if we begin by considering the end result, then we will constantly weigh the end against the means. With small computers, the end alone never justifies the means.

CHARTING TECHNIQUES

Now that we have found out that we will start at the end, let us determine some methods of analyzing ends. Whether you are installing, designing, or purchasing a new computer system, the prime rule to remember is:

- First determine the software.

- Then let the software determine the hardware.

Software is determined by what the end user of the system wants. So, if we can figure out what the user wants, then we will eventually have the system to meet those requirements. To that end there are some general techniques that help define a user's needs.

Charts are a method of graphically outlining a situation. A chart fulfills the dictum that a picture is worth a thousand words. For our purposes, there are three major types of charts:

1. Function charts

2. Decision charts

3. Flowcharts

Function Charts: What has to be done?

This is perhaps the most useful chart in determining requirements in that it is clear, it is concise, and it answers the question, "what must be done?" The most familiar form of this chart is the organizational chart found in any establishment. The chart specifies who expects what from whom.

Even a simple chart of the type shown in Figure 7 makes it clear that the Vice-President of Sales requires information about the office and the market, and that the information has to be pertinent both to the current situation and to long-range analysis.

The major difficulty with function charts is that they do not always include the necessary details. Within systems analysis, numerous methodologies have been developed to force the enumeration of detail.

System Boundaries: How much do
I expect a particular area to handle?

Most techniques follow a similar pattern. The first step is to define the system boundaries. State what the system is expected to handle and

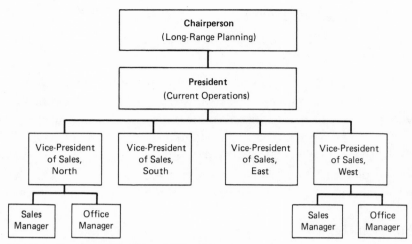

Figure 7 Organizational Chart.

what is outside the scope of the system. This is done by being very general. If we wish to design a system for preparing omelettes, we have to know what the outer limits of the system are. The system may start by assuming all the ingredients are in the cooking areas, or it may be of large scope and include the process of shopping for ingredients, or it may step back further and see purchasing chickens as part of the system.

There is a delightful moment in childhood when system boundaries are first experienced. Teachers ask kids to identify their books by writing their names and addresses in them, and there are always some children who write:

> John Smith
> 1 Happy Lane
> Los Angeles
> California 90405
> The USA
> Earth
> The Galaxy

These children have defined their address system to be all of creation. Some of us use a smaller system that ends at the state and zip code. Others use a slightly larger system that includes the country. A business that never deals with other countries does not need its system boundary to extend that far.

Work Down: Do I have the details of what goes in, what changes occur, and what comes out?

START AT THE TOP AND WORK DOWN

This is another way of saying "start at the end and work backward." Working from the top down forces this point of view by the order of presentation of the charted systems. The first diagram is the general overview (see Figure 8a). Then, with the following pages, you move in on a particular section (see Figure 8b). It's the principle of going from the general to the particular. In a movie, it's the same as going from a general view through a middle view to a close-up.

WHAT THE SYSTEM DOES

In order to derive close-up views that detail sections of the system, certain conventions are used. These conventions turn your attention to what goes on inside the boundaries you have marked out. After all, a system, if it is of any use, must register some kind of change on the elements that go through it. This tells us that a system must have three things: a beginning, a middle, and an end. In other words:

1. Input (source)

2. Transformer (change-maker)

3. Output (result)

In order to force explicit charting, the following rules are considered common sense:

1. Something must be defined as input. You cannot have a system that just transforms and has output. Something cannot come from nothing.

2. Something has to be done to the input to make it output. Otherwise, why put it through the subsystem or system? A

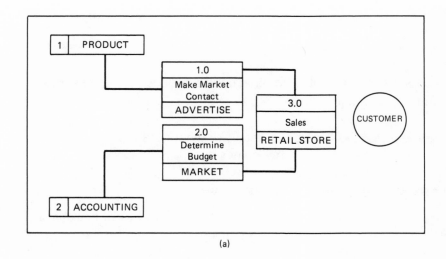

(a)

2.0 DETERMINE BUDGET

2.1
Consult
Inventory

2.2
Consult
Board

2.1
Check
Sales
Forecast

MARKET

(b)

Figure 8 Vice-President of Sales—North. (a) Shows breakdown of Vice-President of Sales' job functions. (b) Shows further breakdown of steps involved in determining budget.

88

transformer can be something as simple as looking at a piece of paper to be sure that it exists. Or, it may involve complex manipulations which require selecting certain input, merging them according to some formula, and passing on the result.

3. Something must be defined as output. You don't want a system where you just pour things into a bottomless pit. Something must come from something.

Decision Tables: Have I defined and set out all the logical rules?

Decision tables elucidate the transformer rules of function charts. They are a method of picturing alternatives, showing when different variables may be used. They show graphically the rules that transformers use.

The expression of a rule in a decision table is the statement of its action and its area of application. The statement is the verb of the sentence and the application is the subject. And, like a sentence, modifiers are used to differentiate possibilities. These modifiers make clear, specific conditions and specific results.

Decision tables are delineated into four parts. The two sections of the top part are read from left to right to determine the specific condition, and the specific result is determined in the sections of the bottom half. A decision table is used to lay out unambiguously all possible permutations of a choice. Every horizontal line of a decision table, whether it be in the top condition section or in the bottom results section, is read one step at a time.

When we lay out a decision table, we want the application column to reflect that the condition or result applies or does not, either exists or does not. Usually, we use a yes/no (Y/N) code with conditions and a "X" indicator for the result that is applicable. A blank means not applicable.

The major point of a decision table is to give you an idea of the number of functions your system must handle. They can be particularly helpful when you are trying to choose prewritten packages. You may want to use an accounts payable package to keep track of your disbursements. It is important to know the number of accounts the accounts payable package can handle. Many small packages have a limit of eight payable disbursements to a chart of accounts. If you require 12, then an 8-limit package is not for you.

Often, a first-time designer of a computer system confuses the idea of something being "easy" with the fact that it can be done by untrained clerical help. Sometimes it is helpful to make up a decision table of a simple clerical action in order to expose the complexity of functions. Consider the task of receiving a monthly payment check against a loan. Part of the check is assigned to paying off the interest and the remainder to paying off the principal balance. A decision table of the general steps involved would look like the example in Figure 9. It is apparent from this chart that more details are required. How do we assess the late charges? Do we send the same letter for a partial payment that is on time as we do for a partial payment that is late?

In order to keep track of the possible entries in a decision table, two rules are applied.

1. Because we are answering Y or N, the possible combinations are 2 raised to the number of conditions. Mathematically, this is written 2^n when $n =$ the number of conditions. So, 2 conditions has 2^2 or 4 possible answers. 3 conditions has 2^3 or 8 possible answers.

2. Since we have now figured out the number of conditions, the next step is to fill in the Y and N answers. Starting with the bottom

Is payment ≥ amount due?	Y	Y	N	N
Is payment on time?	Y	N	Y	N
1. Interest = last month's balance times interest rate	X	X		
2. Principal = interest subtracted from payment	X	X		
3. Current balance = principal subtracted from last month's balance	X	X		
4. Assess late charges		X	X	
5. Send letter			X	X

Figure 9 Payment Decision Table.

condition, alternately write in Y and N. On the next line up, double the Y's and N's. On the third line up, double the Y's and the N's again, so that you have 4 Y's and 4 N's.

Mathematically, we are doing the following:

$$Y = 2^n \text{ where } n = \text{the line number.}$$
$$N = 2^n \text{ where } n = \text{the line number.}$$

And we start making the lines at zero, so

The first line: $Y = 2^0 = 1 = Y$
The second line: $Y = 2^1 = 2 = YY$
The third line: $Y = 2^2 = 4 = YYY$

As you can see, the combinations quickly multiply. This could lead to one enormous chart, or your tables can be broken down into smaller parts. Then, in the results column, you have the option of writing, "go to another table."

The purpose of decision tables is to elucidate and enumerate the things that have to be done in a particular circumstance. When you first lay out a chart or charts, it is better to err on the side of repetition and illogical possibilities.

Even a generalized chart such as the one in the example above can provide us with some important questions for our proposed system. One of the first things we notice is that the results column requires both mathematical manipulations and human communication, a letter. These are two different subsystems of the system, how well do they go together? Remember, the system has to be used by someone, so the questions to ask are:

- What does the user have to do to get the black box to do the mathematics?

- What does the user have to do to get the black box to produce the letter?

A very sophisticated system may only require that the user turn on the machine and make sure the checks to be entered are available.

The user can go away, do other things, and come back later to pick up the envelopes that need to be mailed.

A less sophisticated system may require the constant attendance of the user. Data may have to be input through the keyboard, and then all the computations will be done. After that, the user may have to load another program that generates dunning letters. Then another program may be run to generate mailing labels which then have to be attached to blank envelopes by hand.

Decision tables are used to spell out all the rules necessary to a system. If something meets the conditions of a rule, then certain functions result. In order to avoid driving ourself crazy when trying to determine all the rules, it is often helpful to use the ''other'' rule. If something is part of a system but doesn't meet the conditions you have described, it must be an ''other,'' and the appropriate action will be taken. In our example, ''other'' might have as its action ''speak to accountant'' or ''check with computer vendor'' or ''need more information.''

Use decision tables to list the rules, conditions, and results that make up your system's functions. Also, look at them to see which functions are not being met by the proposed rules and conditions:

Flowcharts: Do I know where everything is going?

Flowcharts have one major function and that is that they diagram a sequence of steps. Very detailed flowcharts are used to work out the step-by-step logical solution to a problem. This type of detail is necessary for programming a particular machine. Less detailed flowcharts are more helpful to the small system designer. After all, there are already many packages available that either perform general business functions or allow the construction and manipulation of data without the bother of keeping track of all the hardware conditions that must be met.

Because flowcharts are designed to force sequential steps, certain conventions are followed. The primary order of a flowchart is from top to bottom. Lines of flow should always have arrows. Rectangles indicate some unambiguous action. Diamond shapes indicate a condition. Circles indicate entry and exit points within the flowchart. Other shapes are used for different input and output mediums and mechanisms. (See Figure 10).

A useful way to utilize flowcharts is to relate them to your decision tables. Each rectangle in a flowchart might indicate a table and each diamond shape might indicate a condition that exists between tables.

A businessperson lists the following things to be computerized:

- General ledger

- Accounts payable

- Monthly reports on state of business

- Ad hoc reports on state of business

Flowcharting a day's use of the computer might look something like Figure 10. Right away we notice that this flowchart tells us that a lot more detail is involved in running the computer than our requirements list shows. Secondly, it frees us to prioritize our decisions.

Prioritizing is built into systems analysis because by definition a system is an expression of order. And order forces us to say that something occurs before, after, or at the same time as something else. Flowcharts can help us get our priorities right.

In the example in Figure 10, the flowchart shows that the first thing we check for are the monthly or ad hoc reports. That may be fine, or we may want to do all the accounting functions first and then move on to additional tasks. Drawing a rough flow chart forces you to make priority decisions.

PERT: Have I figured out when things have to happen and how much time they require?

Priorities are not necessarily inflexible. Like the "other" rule in decision tables, we always have as our first priority: "do we go with our normal priority or are we changing our priorities?" Drawing up a rough flow chart will give you an idea of how many priorities you are willing to handle.

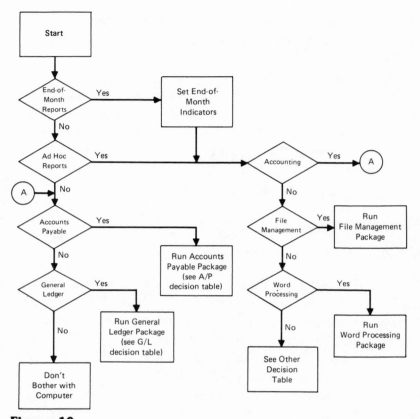

Figure 10

In the late 1950s, the Naval Special Projects Office and Booz, Allen, and Hamilton, a management consultant firm, developed a planning and control technique know as PERT (program evaluation and review technique). Generally, this technique is used for complex projects made up of numerous interrelated activities that have to be completed by a certain time.

PERT defines a system by two time factors: when it takes place and how long it takes. By requiring both of these time elements to be present, it forces prioritization. Then, by looking at the total amount of time allowed to complete an operation, a critical path analysis can tell us which procedures must be done on time and with which ones we have some leeway.

Figure 11

Let's go back to the list of functions we wish to computerize and put in some timing:

- General ledger   = 2 hours
- Accounts payable = 3 hours
- Monthly reports   = 4 hours
- Ad hoc reports   = 2 hours

The times are arbitrary and represent an average amount of time per operation. We know that we must complete the accounts payable for the month before we do the general ledger, and it doesn't matter when we do the reports. We might draw a network like the one in Figure 11. Here our overall timing is 5 hours. However, this type of system assumes that we can do simultaneous jobs, and we must make sure that our black boxes can do multiple functions. We also need to check that we have the personnel to perform multiple functions.

If our system (black box), however, can only do one thing at a time, then we will have to redraw our network (see Figure 12). This assumes

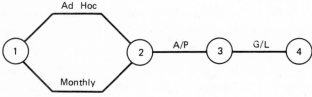

Figure 12

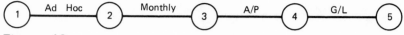

Figure 13

that we can produce ad hoc reports from our monthly reports. If that's not possible, then our network would be Figure 13.

Simple-minded as these examples are, they point up some interesting results. The first diagram tells us that 5 hours is the maximum amount of critical time needed and that we have to do 3 projects simultaneously. The second diagram makes it clear that if we can do only 2 projects simultaneously, we are up to 9 hours. The last diagram makes it clear that we need at least 11 hours to get everything done.

PERT is widely used to both plan and control extensive projects. It is a highly sophisticated and complex tool requiring a great deal of expertise in its use. The design and installation of small computer systems do not require the full force of the PERT methodology. However, the PERT concept of viewing a system as made up of an event and an activity can help the systems analyst identify some of the inbuilt expectations of a proposed system.

Not all black boxes are going to be able to do all their functions at the same time. If you have one terminal and someone is doing word processing, it is not possible to use the machine to do accounting. It is very easy to assume that you wouldn't make such a simple mistake. But small computers, because they are so powerful, may be used by different individuals at different times over the period of a business week. Laying out expected uses in terms of event and activity for this amount of time can be very helpful.

FORMS ANALYSIS

The purpose of any system is to affect something in some way, otherwise there is no point to the system. One way of finding out what goes into a system is to look at what comes out. After all, if you want a list of all customers in a particular geographic area which includes their first name, last name, and initial, you know that you must input that information to begin with. Knowing that it exists, however, is not enough. You also have to know what form it takes.

Forms are the wheels of data processing. The only time anyone pays any attention to them is when they squeak. Most forms are designed by vendors and work so well that we never notice them. Computers, however, not only give us the opportunity to design custom forms, they often demand it.

Whether you are using packaged applications or having software written to your needs, an understanding of forms analysis is essential. *User-friendly* is a term bandied about the computer world to mean a system or device that can be utilized correctly with no special training on the part of the operator, and forms are the guidelines of that friendliness.

Forms are either input or output and can be read directly by a human being. Information printed on paper or on the VDT screen is a form and is subject to human consideration. Information stored on machine readable devices, such as magnetic disks, are subject to machine consideration and are not part of forms analysis.

Data Flow: Do the hand and eye move smoothly?

Some general guidelines for "friendly" information:

1. Data flow should be consistent.

When reading or writing information, we tend to scan either horizontally or vertically. It is difficult and fatiguing to move the eyes in an irregular pattern.

2. Descriptive titles should be exactly that.

If a heading, column, title, or label is not self-explanatory, at least have a record of the meaning easily accessible. (See Chapter 10 on setting up a work and procedures manual.)

3. Adequate space for the information should be provided.

Cramped, tiny letters and numbers are hard to read and lead to errors. When you use additional space, be sure to indicate that there is more. Not everyone automatically turns pages over or brings up the next screen.

INPUT FORMS

An input form is part of the system's procedure; as such, it should be designed to facilitate that procedure. A good form has the following attributes:

It is easy to record information on.   Input errors are minimized. On a printed form, you might show the $ sign to force the user's awareness of what is expected. On a VDT, you might program the field to accept numerals.

The logic of entering information should match the user's expectations. Obvious examples are name and address. For VDT entry, you might put numeric data together to take advantage of the keying rhythms people set up for themselves.

The form asks for what is needed, not more and not less.   Unnecessary information is boring and can lead people to fill in the form in a cursory way. Try to make the opportunity to explain why things are required.

The general way of laying out an input form requires that:

1. Information be filled in.

2. Information be checked off.

With printed forms, make sure there is enough space to fill in. On a VDT, make sure it is easy to hit the right key.

Logic: Does the form help to ensure that the right information is put in the right place at the right time?

Many application programs are written to be *menu driven*. This means that a collection of choices appears on the VDT and you hit a key to indicate your choice. This might lead you to another menu of choices where you again have to hit a key. Consider the following menus:

Main Menu

ENTER SEARCH KEY ABC 1. Find record 2. Edit key	Entering "1" into the system brings up the record with next menu

Find Menu

RECORD KEY ABC 1. Exit 2. Accept	Entering "2" into the system accepts the record you want

Superficially, there is nothing wrong with this approach. However, if you were to sit down and use these two menus for finding a number of records, you would notice the typing discrepancy. First of all, it is fairly safe to assume that the majority of the time that you are looking for a particular record, you wish to accept it for processing. So, you would have to move your finger between the "1" and "2." Not a great distance and seemingly trivial, until you have to process 50 or more records.

The motto of good design is the less work for the user the less strain, and the less strain the fewer errors. Secondly, the logic of the action is continually broken. There will be far more than two menus in a system and the logic to searching is to find and accept. The point is to be consistent within the system and to eliminate unnecessary steps and strain.

When you purchase an application package, check out the input forms. Too often different modules of the system were written at different times, and data entry forms are not consistent. Unless the user demands consideration, the package will continue to be written according to programming aesthetics.

As for quibbling over one key stroke, an example would be an extremely popular piece of business software for a well-known personal computer that had no exit choice. To leave the program, you had to turn off the machine, then reboot. The process was annoying enough that users suggested a modification, and subsequent versions now allow you to quit the program by hitting a single key.

Requirements: Does the form meet the needs of the equipment?

OUTPUT FORMS

An output form should be readable, should contain all the necessary information, and should get to the person who uses it.

Application programs that print forms may require a certain size printer. Accounting programs in particular use wide-carriage printers. Besides making sure you have the correct printer, make sure that it can meet all the demands of the program. Some programs move up and down the page, requiring the printer to respond and the paper to stay aligned. Some programs have been known to interface to only two or three printers.

You don't have to reinvent the wheel when it comes to forms. Most predesigned forms are set up by experienced people, but, as with any part of a computer system, check out the details. Forms are used frequently, requiring enormous amounts of repetitive effort. Keep that in mind when you review them. With forms, it's not the first 100 times that you care about, it's all the times after that.

SECURITY/PRIVACY

There are a number of reasons for securing access to your system. Certain records are confidential to your business, others may be confidential to individuals. A processing situation may arise where you don't want anyone to change a certain record. In any computer system, security means limiting access to data.

Encryption Devices: Have I limited access to the rules of formation?

Information is intelligible only when we understand the form it is stored in. A person whose ideas are expressed in the form of English can not be understood by a person who only knows the rules of French. Knowing the rules by which data was formed enables us to understand the information. Encryption devices are designed to alter stored computer data in such a way that it is unintelligible to anyone who does not have access to the rules of formation. These hardware devices, using unique software algorithms, operate automatically, and the authorized user of the computer system is not even aware of the encryption. In this sense the encryption device is transparent to the programmer and to the end user.

Passwords: Have I limited access to the data?

Different levels of passwords access different levels of the system. The lowest level may allow a user to read only certain fields of data. Another level might allow the user to change fields. And, the highest level would allow the user access to all information, plus the ability to change passwords. This highest level can come in handy when dealing with a disgruntled employee. It is not uncommon for an angry individual to erase or confuse your data.

Locks: Have I limited access to the equipment?

ELECTRONIC FILE LOCKS

You can specify that certain files only be read and not written to. This is used when many people might have access to the same information. It could be disastrous if a monetary payment is erased before it is recorded for the day. This can happen if more than one clerk is transacting with the file at the same time. Usually, these types of locks are taken care of by the operating system and do not concern the end user.

MECHANICAL LOCKS

Many CPUs come with a start key. This is like the ignition lock on your car, and it serves the same purpose. Lacking this, keep your equipment, particularly your CPU, in an area that can be locked.

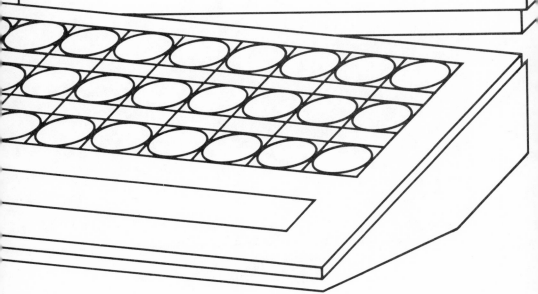

6 LOOKING AT YOUR ENVIRON-MENT

6 LOOKING AT YOUR ENVIRONMENT

Computer systems occupy space and need attention. Plan for the needs of the machine and for the needs of the people who run the system.

I. THE RIGHT PLACE AND THE RIGHT PEOPLE MAKE IT ALL WORK

II. EQUIPMENT NEEDS
   1. Environment: Does the machinery have enough clean space and clean power?
   2. Storage Space: Have areas been set aside for reference manuals, supplies, and backup?
   3. The Flow of Data: Are there areas for the physical input and output of the computer?

4. Operator Comfort: Have the sources of irritability and fatigue been checked?

III. PERSONNEL
1. Operations: Does the individual running the system show patience, perseverance, and attention to detail?
2. Training: Does the individual learning the system know how to study?

THE RIGHT PLACE AND THE RIGHT PEOPLE MAKE IT ALL WORK

It is an observable phenomenon that many people are intimidated by computers. There are many reasons that computers have a bad reputation:

"They are cold, merciless machines that replace human beings."

"Computers are too difficult to understand; you need to be a math or science major in order to use one."

"Computers operate so fast I don't have time to think."

"Computers are expensive. If I enter the wrong information, I could turn it all to mush."

These are just a few of the spoken and unspoken attitudes people have when first confronted with computers.

Some of these objections can be overcome, some can be planned for, and some will just have to be accepted. A computer is only a tool and is not necessarily for everybody. Not everybody has to be able to make furniture in order to utilize a table.

Objections raised against computers are neither silly nor uncommon. Large corporations have found that the installation of a terminal or small computer in a major executive's office does not necessarily lead to better management information. "Computeritis" is a reaction that has to be coped with.

Computers do not replace human beings, they replace certain human tasks. It is foolish to deny this. If a machine has been installed to be a time saver, what will be done with the time saved? Hopefully it will be used to get to things you never quite had the time to do before. It is important to address the fears a computer may generate.

Computers are too difficult to understand.   Certainly to design and build a computer is a complex, highly skilled craft. But very few of us can build the cars we drive. Making use of a tool is not the same as making the tool.

Computers are expensive.   True, but in the long run, so is everything. As long as you pay attention to what you're doing, you won't break the machine. You may waste time, but you cannot physically hurt the machine by entering data from the keyboard.

It all adds up to a willingness to play with the system. Play, after all, is one of the ways we become proficient within a set of constraints (see Chapter 1). The person who gets the most use out of a small computer is the one who is willing to play with it. The person who plays with a computer will not be intimidated by the machine and will in fact enjoy utilizing it.

Play here refers to an attitude on the part of the user and the machine. Playing games on a computer is using the machine in a function other than as a business tool. To play with computers is not the same as playing games with computers. And people who like to play games on machines do not necessarily work well with computers in a business environment.

It is axiomatic that the most expensive ongoing cost of any computer system is personnel. This is particularly true with small computers. A minimal, workable system, including hardware and software, can be put together for under $3000. This is a one-time cost easily amortized over a 5-year period.

In a small business of 1 to 20 employees, what is the cost per hour of the person operating the system? If the secretary is busy running the accounting program, then the dictation will have to wait. Too often a business will install a small computer on the grounds that the typist/receptionist/general helper can operate it while answering the phone and performing other duties. A highly skilled secretary acting as a data entry clerk is overpaid as a clerk and underutilized as a secretary. The cost to the business is the waste in salary and a poor performance from a frustrated employee.

The point is that it pays to make the computer system easy to operate and cost-effective in terms of personnel. System requirements dictate physical and personnel needs. Computer machinery cannot just be placed anywhere and left to whoever has a free moment.

EQUIPMENT NEEDS

At first glance, small computers which are small enough to fit on a desk would not seem to require much space planning. However, as with any piece of equipment, it is utilized most efficiently if its physical characteristics are set up to help rather than hinder its operation.

There are three major areas of concern:

1. The physical requirements of the hardware.

2. The flow of data.

3. Operator comfort.

Environment: Does the machinery have
enough clean space and clean power?

On the whole, small computers are not physically dependent. However, there are some things that should be kept in mind.

Ordinary line voltage is fine, but make sure that you have enough outlets to handle all your pieces of equipment. All equipment requires grounded outlets. Often equipment with two-pronged connectors are polarized. A simple solution is to purchase a bar extension with three or four outlets. Be sure to check the manufacturer's requirements for the order of turning equipment on and off.

A computer memory is subject to fluctuations in line voltage, so certain environments may require the use of a surge suppressor. Usually this is only necessary in areas where there may be a sudden, heavy demand for electricity. If you are using a small computer in a high-density industrial or business park, you may want to consider a surge suppressor.

Magnetic memory is by nature susceptible to electrical discharge, such as static. Many office carpets are heavy generators of static, and the computer needs to be shielded from this. Antistatic mats that go under the operator's feet are readily available.

Whatever computer is purchased make sure that the CPU has adequate ventilation. Small computer equipment is air cooled and relies on the free flow of air. Temperature buildups can affect operation. If your computer is the type that has a main board into which you can plug additional boards, it may be necessary to purchase a small fan to circulate the air. Additional boards can generate enough heat to cause intermittant processing problems.

It is wise to keep the machinery in as much of a clean-air environment as possible. Putting a small computer hard disk under a table directly on the carpet is not a good idea. At the very least, raise the machinery off the carpet. A good rule of thumb is that if you wouldn't like to be breathing the environment neither would your small computer.

The only other concern in terms of pollutants is floppy disks. These disks are sensitive and do not respond well to cigarette ash, coffee, or fingerprints on the recording surface. Because they are a magnetic recording medium, they can be affected by strong magnetic fields. It is important to keep them stored in the paperlike envelope they come in. This protects the exposed read-write slot when the disk is not in use.

The printer has certain physical requirements with respect to its use of paper. When using continuous form paper, there must be a clear run for the paper between the supply pile and the take-up pile. Different printers have different requirements. Tension or distortion of the paper before it reaches the print head can cause misalignment at the paper feed, resulting in paper jams. The important thing is to check how much space the computer needs when it is operating and loaded with paper. It is not always possible to put your printer flat on the table and flush with the wall.

Storage Space: Have areas been set aside
for reference manuals, supplies, and backup?

Besides the hardware, there are associated objects that must be considered in space planning. An area near the computer and easily reached by the operator must be set aside for all the reference material that comes with the computer system. Every additional piece of software or hardware will come with its own reference sheet or manual, and these must be kept together in one place.

It can be extremely frustrating and expensive if a year after you have set up your system you purchase a new piece of equipment that requires some software configuration and the manual for the CPU is not around. Not all hardware and software works with all other hardware and software, and most of the computer errors made by humans occur because people overestimate the ability of the machine.

The following is a list of storage equipment and requirements for a typical small computer:

1. Next to the equipment

a. A small bookcase, shelves, or some separate area is needed for the manuals.

b. Holders of some variety, plastic boxes, or metal boxes are needed to keep your external magnetic storage. They should have dividers so that your programs are separate from your data disks. They should be easily available to the operator while at the computer.

Care must be taken so that the media will not be exposed to magnetic fields, cigarette ash, spilled coffee, or the hazard of falling on the floor. Have physically separate storage containers for your backup copies of both programs and data.

2. Nearby access

The computer needs supplies: paper for the printer, binders to hold reports, fresh magnetic storage media, ribbons for the printer, spare point heads, different colored labels for magnetic media. Space must be set aside for the storage of these items.

3. Separate location

You must and should have backup copies of all your programs and all your data (see Chapter 7). The purpose of having backup copies is to guard yourself against the unexpected loss of business data. You could spend a day typing in a 20-page report, using your machine as a word processor. The next day, someone decides to use the computer to update the inventory system, and they use your data disk by mistake. Murphy's law goes into operation. A great deal of time, anguish, and aggravation is saved if a duplicate is sitting in a safe place. And the emphasis is on "safe." It is not enough to copy your disks and keep them with your other disks. It is much better to keep a physically separate backup file. Better than that is to keep your backup in another room in a fireproof safe. Many people who run small businesses keep their backup at home. Perhaps the best procedure is to rent a safety deposit box and keep your backup in the vault of your bank.

Backup must be made to protect against loss by human error, machine error, or natural catastrophe!

The Flow of Data: Are there areas for the physical input and output of the computer?

The physical demands of the computer extend to the type of use that will be asked of it. Obviously, a system that is used mainly for quick information retrieval on a VDT screen has different environmental requirements than a machine that is producing a great deal of printed matter and/or accepting a great deal of information from the keyboard (see Chapter 3).

At this level, our concern is with the physical elements of input and output. A great deal of input at the keyboard requires:

1. A comfortable work environment for the operator.

2. A place to store the original input information while it is being worked on.

3. A place to store the original information after it has been entered.

Not to belabor the obvious, but there must be a space or tray to hold the material to be entered, and there must be a space or tray to hold the material already entered. It is very easy when you are entering a lot of information to get mixed up or forget to enter a record. Consider the following scenario.

It is the end of the month and it is time to update your customer list. Because of one thing or another, 50 new customers have to be added. The person who is adding the new names to the file is doing it between 11 A.M. and 2 P.M. This happens to coincide with the lunch hour, and this person is the only one in the office. Then the phone rings . . . . It is very easy to put a piece of paper in the wrong pile. And, although there are other controls (see Chapter 7), one of the best controls is to prevent it from happening in the first place.

A great deal of output at the printer requires

1. A good flow of paper.

2. Storage of the printed output.

3. Distribution of the output on a timely basis.

Computers are notorious paper generators. Therefore, two areas should always be looked at when you are considering a potential report:

1. Is this report necessary?

2. If this report is necessary, who sees it, where is it kept, and for how long?

HEAVY USE OF THE VDT

First of all, make sure that all those people who will be viewing the screen can see it properly. It is possible to attach multiple monitors to a single CPU. Alternatively, the keyboard and the monitor can be placed on a lazy susan to make them accessible from different sides of a desk.

The amount of constant viewing time is the determining factor in choosing between a black-and-white and a green VDT screen. Concentrated work for many hours in front of a green screen can cause fatigue. There are no hard and fast rules for choosing a television or a black-and-white monitor or a green monitor. Consider, however, the story of the hi-fi enthusiast who spends $1000 on equipment to reproduce the music and saves $50 by buying an inexpensive stylus. In order to save $50, the enthusiast is sacrificing irreplaceable recordings. The analogy is that in the computer world the VDT is one of the direct links between the machine and the operator and can directly affect the quality of the output.

Operator Comfort: Have the sources of irritability and fatigue been checked?

This is the area where the physical requirements of the hardware and the flow of data come together. It is particularly important with high-level data entry to take operator comfort into account. Errors are a common cause of system problems. We all know how easy it is if we're late and in a hurry to misfile something. The speed and power of a small computer can compound such an error a thousandfold.

The following points are important when placing the computer in the work environment.

The chair must be comfortable and provide firm leg and back support.

The height of the keyboard is similar to the placement of a typewriter. Relaxed shoulders and an easy hand motion are desirable.

The VDT should be at eye level. Having to look up at the VDT causes strain on the neck muscles, which leads to tension, which leads to fatigue, which leads to errors.

There are only two pieces of computer equipment whose operational noise may cause a problem. These are printers and hard disk drives.

A high-speed impact printer producing a long report can have an annoying machine-gun sound quality. If the printer cannot be moved, sound boxes can be purchased. Again, make sure there is a baffle box available for your choice of printer.

Hard disks operate at high speed in their own sealed environment. Some of them emit a high-pitched whine that can be very disturbing. As they are designed to be on continuously, over a period of hours this noise can be extremely annoying and disruptive to work. Try to find a nearby area that can be acoustically isolated for this piece of hardware. Keep in mind the manufacturer's distance limitations, if any, between the CPU and the hard disk.

PERSONNEL

Whoever runs the computer must know how to operate it. This is not as self-evident as it sounds, in that specific knowledge is required to handle certain hardware requirements.

Many small computers are easy to attach peripherals to because they are designed for use on a modular basis. Taking the cover off of a computer does not necessarily turn off the power, however. The danger of not turning all power off at every device is that, besides the possibility of giving yourself a shock, you can short-circuit your computer when removing a peripheral device connector. It happens all the time, and replacement costs can run into hundreds of dollars. Also, different peripherals may have precedence requirements in being powered up or down. Ignorance of these can cause the loss of data.

Running a program may not require detailed machine operation, but no matter how simple or user-friendly the system, there have to be procedures unique to the equipment and your business's use of it. (See Chapter 10 about setting up a work and procedures manual.) There is nothing more frustrating than to be in the middle of running a packaged program that asks for 132-column printing and your printer hasn't been set up for it.

The friendliest of computer systems requires 10 to 20 hours of familiarity. Keep in mind that we are talking about an entire system. Even if hardware is dedicated to a particular function and as many variables as possible are eliminated, the operator must have the confidence to recover from an error or to recreate the backups when data is irretrievably lost.

Operations: Does the individual running the system show patience, perseverance, and attention to detail?

The following attributes are helpful in operating computers and running programs:

1. Patience

The individual must be willing to try the same thing over again and again.

2. Perseverance

Sometimes one step in a sequence needs to be changed. It can take a number of tries to find this out.

3. Detail

Attention to detail is critical. Computers accept things as they are, not as the operator assumes.

PATIENCE

It is obvious that systemized work flow becomes routine. An interesting phenomenon that accompanies the use of a computer is a foreshortening of temporal perception. The most common example of this occurs during record searches.

Assume that a company has a customer file of 1000 records that they deal with manually. If it is decided to make a list of all customers in the last year who spent more than $1000 with the firm, this report could take 2 or more days to prepare. Using a small computer, the report may take only 30 minutes from start to finish.

On the surface, the time savings are enormous. Unfortunately, it can be very boring sitting around while the computer is manipulating data. Operators begin to complain about the slowness of the machine. Boredom leads to inattention, and trivial mistakes are made through lack of attention to detail. Murphy's law comes into effect, and the wrong report arrives in the wrong place at the wrong time.

The solution to the problem is twofold:

1. Make sure that the person who is running the system knows enough about the system to appreciate what it is doing. This person should like playing with gadgets.

2. Make sure the person has responsibilities other than just sitting around watching the machine run. This last point is probably not a problem; the difficulty is making sure that in leaving the computer system and coming back to it the person continues to pay attention to detail.

PERSEVERANCE

Sometimes the best way to solve a computer error is to repeat everything leading up to the error. Until the operator can see exactly the sequence of events that occurred, the problem, regardless of the solution, may not be clear. It takes a great deal of perseverance to step through a system detail by detail. Remember that the solution to a problem does not ensure that it will not happen again.

The solution to the immediate error is only the beginning of the job. If the error is causing a problem of effective magnitude (in other words, it is not something that you can live with), then the steps leading up to the situation must be discovered and if not corrected, then documented. The following example is fairly typical.

Computers sort by character. A before B, B before C, and so on. One of the characters in any computer code is the blank. A blank space is as much a character as a letter, number, or special symbol. So, if a blank is inserted or left out of a name, that name is not the same as if the blank was not inserted or left out. Smith blank & blank Jones is not the same as Smith&Jones. Information filed under the first heading will not necessarily be available under the second heading.

Another instance: A software package uses a name as the identifying search key. The name is requested on the VDT in the following format: NAME_____. The information is to be filled in where the dashes are. If, for example, the country name CANADA is typed in, the record associated with NAME is retrieved by typing in CANADA when NAME_____ appears on the screen. But if in entering the data, the space bar had been hit by mistake, the unique set of characters BLANK C A N A D A may not be referenced by subsequently asking for C A N A D A.

The problems of data entry can be frustrating and tedious. A well-designed system will, to the best of its ability, check the "reasonableness" of data (see Chapter 7). In other words, if the system asks for a date, it will expect a numeral for the particular day between 1 and 31. However, if July 8 is entered instead of July 9, the system will not know that a 9 should have been entered and not an 8.

It is not impossible to set up such checks, but every solution in the real world represents a trade-off of priorities. Packages are built according to these considerations: the cost of memory versus available operating systems, the available pool of programming talent, and the deadline to bring the product to market.

DETAIL

This is the catchall category that holds patience and perseverance together. Anyone who plays with computers must have an *eye* for detail. It is very easy to look at Mississippi on a VDT and miss an "s." The computer may require that you address it using a pound sign (#); it is easy to use a quotation mark (") instead. PR#1 doesn't look that different from PR"1.

A system may have 2 disk drives available and a software package may use drive 1 for the data disk 9 times out of 10. On the tenth time, if the data disk is placed in drive 1 instead of drive 2, the system will write files to the wrong disk. Later, when the system needs those files, the result is confusion. The system will tell you the file can't be found, and you know very well it was created not too long ago.

The error could be a faulty disk drive, a bug in the operating system, a bug in the application program, or a human error during one of the setup sequences. It can require a great deal of patience, perseverance, and attention to detail to track down the problem.

Training: Does the individual learning
the system know how to study?

Any system that is acquired should come with some training time. For one reason or another, this does not always happen. Perhaps the system is purchased through the mail. Or what is considered adequate training by the salesperson is not enough for the eventual operator. Also, after your system is in place, you may have changes in personnel. New people will need to be trained, and the original vendor may no longer exist or be capable of ongoing support. Some things are just beyond control.

What the user can control is the flip side of training—learning. There is nothing esoteric about learning to operate a computer system. Like anything else, it just takes time and practice. Using some or all of the following steps can help you learn a new system:

1. Read the instructions.

2. Set up the test data.

3. Make a copy of your test data and store it in a safe place.

4. Take notes on what you are doing as you go along.

5. Refer to the instructions.

6. Make conscious errors.

1. Read the instructions.

This can be one of the most difficult habits to inculcate in yourself or in your staff. Nothing, however, can take the place of reading the information that is supplied by the manufacturer. The following is a suggested outline for approaching the material:

a. Familiarize yourself with what has been supplied.

    (1) Determine what instructions and manuals have been given. A manual may be written as a tutorial, a reference, or a combination of the two.

    (2) Determine the subject matter of each particular manual. Commands involving the software operating system will not be found in the reference manual for the supplied programming language.

    (3) Become familiar with the table of contents.

    (4) If there is an index, get a feel for its level of detail.

    (5) Determine what information has been put in appendixes.

b. Read the bulk of the manual.

    (1) The first time through, do a quick skim as though you were reading a novel. Don't worry about terms and ideas that you don't understand. Just go through the entire manual at least once.

    (2) If the manual is of the tutorial type, and not a reference manual, follow the tutorial. Use the examples in the manual, then you can compare your results to the book. This is not the time to experiment. Take a 5-minute break for every hour you spend with the computer and the tutorial.

    Keep in mind that the object of the exercise is proficiency with as well as understanding of the system. A so-called user-friendly system can be learned in an hour. However, it may take from 5 to 15 hours to become proficient. Spread the proficiency curve over a number of days. It is better to spend 5 hours at the machine spread over 3 days than 5 hours in 1 day.

(3) Computer systems generate manuals the way empty closets generate hangers. Know which ones you must read, which ones you should look at and which ones you can ignore until you need them.

2. Set up test data

Do not start learning or using a new system and expect it to yield correct results the first time through. If it does, it's a bonus. To begin with, use test data. Test data should be as close to real or "live" data as possible. The closer the better.

If you are using the computer as a word processor to formulate letters, pull out 5 to 10 letters from your files. Make sure that the letter layouts that are unique to your organization can be handled by the system you've chosen.

Some companies require letters with a great deal of numeric information, other companies have special character requirements. How easy is the tabbing? If multipage material is being prepared and normally goes through many editing cycles, how well can the system cope with such a situation?

In other words, if you are preparing a 25-page report, it's not enough to test the system's capabilities on a two-paragraph letter. Admittedly, the criteria for choosing a word processing system should have taken these questions into account. But, there is a difference in knowing the capabilities of a system and becoming proficient in its use.

The best way to determine if a system is working correctly is to use your own company's past data as a test. If you are buying stereo equipment, you would test it by using music of your choice, not the manufacturer's.

A word processing system was used as an example above because it is seemingly so simple and obvious, it shouldn't need testing. The rule is that anything that is going to be used in your business must be tested. When it comes to a series of programs as complex as an accounting system, they must be tested over a period of time. (See Chapter 9 under Parallel Testing.)

3. Make copies of test data

In the best of all possible worlds, test data is a copy of live data. If the test data has been created, make a copy before any changes are made. Make copies of the test data at selected intervals and keep all copies. The objective at this time is to gain proficiency in the use of the system and to keep track of the system's flow.

The accounts receivable module of a general ledger system may offer 5 to 10 functions. It is necessary for the operator to become familiar with the daily order of running and to be aware of which section is dependent on having run a previous section.

It is not always apparent to new users, for example, that most accounts receivable systems require the building of a customer record before the first and subsequent customer orders can be entered. Quite logically, users new to the system may assume that the computer gets the customer information from the order they are entering. Most systems do not.

4. Take notes

Note taking is perhaps the most neglected art in operating computers. Notes can be used as mnemonic devices to learn the system. They can act as maps and save you from going over the same terrain again and again. And, of course, they provide a record for when things go wrong. At the very least, when a call is made to the supplier, information will be available to help track down the errors.

5. Refer to the instructions

If something doesn't work in the expected way, refer to the documentation. The operator must develop the habit of looking up answers. Too often, a system is underutilized or misused because the operator isn't comfortable with looking up a particular alternative. Familiarity with the documentation and with the underlying logic of the system is necessary for ease of reference.

6. Make errors

It is important to know what you cannot do with the system. Days can be lost because someone thought, "the computer will do it." Additionally, first-time users need to gain confidence and overcome the "sweaty palms" syndrome. As long as adequate backup exists, entering garbage from the keyboard cannot hurt the machinery nor the system.

7 HOUSE-KEEPING

7 HOUSEKEEPING

Why things have to be the way they are. Determining how to keep your finger on the pulse of the system.

I. HOUSE RULES KEEP IT ALL RUNNING SMOOTHLY

II. THINGS THAT MUST BE DONE
1. Audit Trails: Can I keep track of everything that is going on?
2. Rectifying Mistakes: What steps can I use to get things back on the right track?
3. Project Management: Have I determined when everything has to be done?

4. Types of Files: What do I want to do to my data?
5. Record Retention: How long before I can throw it out?

III. THINGS TO GUARD AGAINST
1. Data Checking: Am I sure that the system is getting reasonable input?
2. Physical Loss of Data: Have I guarded against accidents?

HOUSE RULES KEEP IT ALL RUNNING SMOOTHLY

One of the most complex systems that all of us use without consciously seeing it as such is our home. Our home environment is the base of our daily lives. Certain things have to be done to maintain ourselves: our clothes must be washed, food provided, bathrooms kept clean, furniture dusted. The busier we are, the more we delegate these numerous but necessary chores. Housekeeping ranges from the once-a-week cleanup of the organized single person to a full-time position occupied by a salaried employee. Housekeeping is the essential management of the basic home environment to ensure that the home can be utilized by those occupying it.

The electronic data processing world uses the term *housekeeping* to mean the same thing. If we view a complete system as an environment designed to support some type of existence, then computer systems and "homes" (human operating machine environments) have a great deal in common.

In order for both to operate efficiently, the floors must be swept, the lamps must work, the garbage must be collected. Housekeeping makes sure our house and our computer system are in order.

The law of entropy tells us that order decays toward disorder and not the other way around. And, unfortunately, computer systems are as subject to the law of entropy as are our houses.

Keeping order in our homes falls mainly into two categories: (1) Things that must be done and (2) things that must be guarded against. In a home, the things that must be done range from paying the electricity bill on time to throwing out the garbage. Things that must be guarded against range from underpaying or overpaying bills to making sure that one black shoe and one dark-brown shoe are not worn as a pair.

These examples are obvious because we take our own sophisticated systems for granted. Try to remember a time when housekeeping was not simple. Do you remember how hard it was at first to tie a bow? As a child, everything had to be spelled out for you; the same is true of the computer system. Somewhere, someplace, things have to be spelled out.

Fortunately, we only have to make sure that certain main areas are covered. Software packages and the hardware will often take care of the details. When we check with the housekeeper about the state of the living room, it is often enough to ask, "is the room clean?" We do not have to ask specifically, "is the floor swept," or "are the chairs in order?" The more sophisticated a computer system is, the fewer detailed questions need to be asked about the running of it.

THINGS THAT MUST BE DONE

Audit trails are the spoor left by the data's passage. The hunter or detective who comes afterward determines action and number. Like the hunter in the forest who must look at broken branches and footprints to be able to state, "Four elephants and an orangutan passed by here before noon," so must the auditors of the system be able to state, "5000 data elements passed this point before 2 P.M."

Audit Trails: Can I keep track of everything that is going on?

Audit trails are designed to register the path of data in a computer system. If 5000 data elements are expected to pass a certain point at a certain time, a total of 500 would be worth investigating.

Audit trails are expected of accounting systems, but they are necessary to any system. The efficiency of small computers can often make us neglect the obvious. If, for example, the system is designed to be used mainly as an electronic filing cabinet, and the company has 1000 customers that it keeps track of over the period of a year, it is extremely helpful to keep track of what was processed and when. After all, an error might not show up until the end of the year, the time it takes to completely process every record at least once.

This brings us to a very important statement: the first-time rule. Its two corollaries are the last-time rule and the every-other-time rule.

The first-time rule states that things are always a little bit special the first time around. It's like the first time you kiss someone: not everything is in place, you need to make adjustments for your hands, find the right angle to tilt your head. The first time is not the same as every other time.

With a computer system, the same thing holds true. Let's look at a simple loan payment system. The setup is as follows. An amount of money is borrowed; let's identify it as the *principal amount*. The person who borrows the money agrees to pay back the money according to the following rules:

1. A monthly payment will be made.

2. Part of the monthly payment will go toward interest.

3. Part of the monthly payment will be deducted from the principal.

4. Each month's interest is computed on the last month's principal balance.

The computer system is made up of the following steps, which occur in order and define the fields:

1. *Principal amount* is the field that holds the original amount paid.

2. *Total collected* is the field that holds the monthly payment agreed on.

3. *Interest paid* is the field that stores the interest total for that month. This field is defined as last month's principal balance times the monthly interest rate.

4. *Principal paid* is defined as the total collected minus the interest paid.

5. *Last month's principal balance* is equal to the principal amount minus the total principal payments to date.

6. *Principal payment to date* holds the principal accumulated plus this month's principal.

Let's enter a principal amount and total collection. We are not making a payment, just entering basic amounts. The first time through this computer system sequence, the fields would yield the following results:

1. Principal amount = $10,000.

2. Total collection = $105 (monthly payment).

3. This month's payment = 0.

4. Interest paid = 0 times the monthly interest rate or 0×0.0067 percent.

5. Principal paid = 0.

6. Last month's principal balance = $10,000.

7. Principal payment to date = 0.

8. Interest rate = yearly rate divided by 12.

These are the results we want. However, let's reverse 4 and 5 and put number 8 at the top so that our list looks like the following. Remember, the machine operates in order of instruction sequence.

1. Interest rate

2. Principal amount

3. Total collection

4. Last month's principal balance

5. Interest paid

6. Principal payments to date

7. This month's payment

8. Principal paid

Now, when we enter amounts the first time, we will get the following results:

1. Interest rate = 0.0067 percent.

2. Principal amount = $10,000.

3. Total collection = $105.

4. Last month's principal balance = $10,000.

5. Interest paid = $66.67.

6. Principal paid = 0.

Because the interest rate comes before last month's principal balance, the computer came up with a figure other than zero. If the interest rate is at the end of the list, then the first time through the machine multiplies the figure in the principal balance by what's in the interest rate field. But, because the computer hasn't figured that out yet, that field is at zero. And, anything times zero is zero.

This is a typical first-time programming problem, and most programs are written to take this kind of situation into account. But, although programs and packages can and are written to handle the first-time rules of computers, they cannot be expected to know the unique first-time rules of your business.

The first-time rule should not stop you from purchasing a system, but it should make you aware of operational limitations. The following example shows how the first-time rule is applied to system flow.

The purchased hardware includes an 80-column dot-matrix printer with a compressed print feature. *Compressed print* means that 132 characters can be typed in the same amount of space as 80 by compacting the width of each character. This feature is only available under program control.

The software you have purchased prints reports in 132 columns, but does not send out controls to the printer. A separate, subsidiary program has been written that initializes your printer to 132 characters.

Lastly, the printer's normal mode is 80 characters and you can get back to it by turning the printer off and then back on. In other words, turning off the power to the printer cancels any programmed switches.

With these constraints in mind, the first-time rule implies that you had better run your printer utilization program before you run your report generator. Consider the fact that some of your reports may be only 80 characters and placed on preprinted forms, so you might first want do as many 132 reports as you can. After all, to reset the printer to 132 after you have gone back to 80 requires leaving the current program, running the 132-print program, reloading the application, and getting back to where you left off.

The first-time rule is not a hard-and-fast thing. Rather, it is an aid in dealing with the order of the computer world. After all, constraints can only be handled if they can be recognized.

Having identified the first-time record helps the bulk of the remaining records by exclusion. And it is helpful in a system to keep some track of this vast flow of information. Subtotals and grand totals are common means of doing this in any business system. Computer systems are no different.

If the majority of your accounts payable average $100 a month and you pay 10 vendors, you'd expect a subtotal of $1000. If the figure was $650 or $2000, you'd wait to check. But, if you weren't given the capability of seeing the subtotal break, you would have to accept the system on faith—not a good idea.

Audit trails include record counts, totals of selected fields, and header and trailer records. All of these may be used by the system internally to monitor input or externally to monitor output.

An internal audit trail is often associated with *transaction dating*. This means that the system will record the date on which some change, any change, was made to a record. It won't tell you what change has been made, just that something was done to the record.

Header records are the first records in a file and serve to identify the file in some manner. Often, these are used programmatically outside of the user's control to identify the file being used.

Some packages, however, have been known to assume that the file that is online is the one that is expected. This can result in major problems. The most common is that when the file is written to, existing necessary information is destroyed and the file is garbled. Additionally, as the information has been written to the wrong place, it is not in the right place. This will cause all sorts of problems later on when the system goes looking for essential information.

A solution to this type of problem is to make the first record of the file a header file. If your records are indexed by an alphanumeric name, you might call the first record "AA-HEADER," or even "00000." And you might fill in the subsequent fields with pertinent information. This could include the date the file was created, the date the file was last used, the name of the file, and an indication of necessary associated files. Information in the header record would reference the work and procedures manual (see Chapter 10).

Trailer records are the last records in the file and serve to summarize the state of the file. This record may contain such information as the total number of records in the file, the total number of changes (transactions) made since the previous date the file was used, or even the initials of who last looked at the file.

Many packages will automatically check that the correct file is online and provide for other safeguards. It is for the user to decide if the system requires additional checks and balances. Obviously, with a system where only one or two people actively use the equipment, extensive user audit trails may not be necessary. If three or more people are changing records on a daily or even weekly basis, it is worth considering the use of additional audit trails.

Consider the case of a software package, whether it is an accounting package or a data base management package, that automatically dates each transaction to a record with the date used to sign on to the system. Let's say that John and Mary sign on to the machine in the morning and change 50 records. They work part time and leave by noon. At two o'clock, Howard and Nancy sign on to the machine and change 45 records. Just before leaving for the day, Howard runs a report listing all the records by the current date. If the afternoon shift and the morning shift signed on with the same date, all 95 records will be printed out. But what about the possibility of one of the groups signing on with the wrong date? Possible solutions to this problem might be to (1) have each team print a list of its transactions before signing off, (2) leave the machine on all day so that the date for the day remains constant, or (3) have an audit trail record for each team, that they create, which records their total transactions for the day.

Rectifying Mistakes: What steps can I use to get things back on the right track?

Audit trails may be designed to keep us on the right path, but every system must incorporate the means of getting back on course when things go astray. Mistakes range from entering an incorrect character, misspelling a name, entering $5000 instead of $500, to getting through half a year's processing and finding out that a piece of information was initially wrong or not included. You cannot plan for everything, but you can plan on errors being made.

Many software packages will provide edit features that enable you to reenter data. If you put in the wrong address while adding a record, you might be able to change the line, or you might have to delete the entire record and enter it again. Sometimes the edit feature is available on a line-by-line basis when a record is first created, but fixed after you have entered the record.

Some packages utilize their editing capabilities to update numeric fields which will be used for certain computations. However, the package might not recognize that you have entered the edit mode to change an address, not enter a monthly payment. Saving the new address might initiate the monthly computation. In this case, to change an address you would have to indicate in the work and procedures manual that the entire record must be deleted and then added back in.

Mistakes need to be rectified, both at the time they are committed and at a later point in time. It is usually the attempt to rectify errors at a later date that causes the most grief. Certainly when buying packages, you must ask for reentry points. With the system itself, there must be times in the work flow when errors can be corrected. Error reentry goes from the system level all the way down to the item level.

At the system level, if something has gone wrong, you can return to the previous best case by going to your backup files. At the item level, you must have the capability to enter information that is correct to both the item and its position in time. In other words, it is not enough to just delete the item and add a new one. What if computations have been done on that item for the past 6 months? What running totals are affected by this change, and can they be brought back into line? If the package cannot register the change, then documentation must be filled out and attention must be drawn to the deviation. The work and procedures manual would be the place to note all this.

If the mistake requires documentation, the following points must be covered:

1. A description of the mistake

2. What was changed to rectify the mistake

3. The date of the change

4. Who made the change

5. What other, if any, parts of the system are affected

6. A notation on the master index that an error of documentable magnitude has been fixed

It is important that whoever runs the system, whether it be on a daily basis or on one off occasion, be aware that the system has had some changes made to it. Too often an error is rectified and the correction documented in the section devoted to errors, but it is not indicated in the running instructions. Some months later, something out of the ordinary occurs because of the error adjustment. The current user has gone exactly by the running instructions and does not understand why things are not as they are documented.

Project Management: Have I determined
when everything has to be done?

Project management is the art of making sure that everything gets done on time. Scheduling is the key. See Chapter 5 for a discussion of management scheduling and applicable tools for designing a new system. In housekeeping, project management for the user entails documenting the job stream and creating necessary reports and documentation.

Small computers by design are user-friendly and therefore require more involvement on the part of the end user. Any time the user interacts with a small computer, it should be seen as part of a project. Projects can be a single action or job or can be made up of multiple actions or jobs. That is, someone may be just using the computer to update files, or they may be generating reports that require the running of several jobs. Whatever the user does, certain minimum guidelines should be considered.

Document what must be done in what sequence in order for the user to gain access to the system (see Figure 14):

1. Order of powering up the equipment

2. Which projects must be completed before running the current one

3. Date of the most recent master files that can be used

4. Which system date, if any, is to be entered

5. Things to have ready before entering the main phase
   a. Initialized discs
   b. Printer set to necessary character width

6. How to take backup

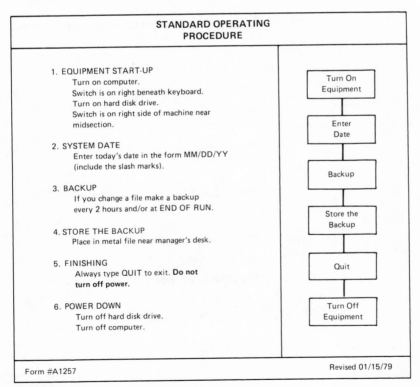

Figure 14

7. When to take backup

8. Where to store backup

9. Exiting the system gracefully

10. Order of powering down the equipment

If the system is already up and running, then only part of this sequence applies during a project. But, during any one workday with the computer, all of the above must be covered; a workday being defined as the time the equipment is turned on to when it is turned off.

1. Order of powering up the equipment

Certain pieces of hardware require that other pieces be turned on before them. CPUs should be powered up before hard disks.

2. Which projects must be completed before running the current one

In an accounting system, you must usually close the receivables for the month before moving on to the general ledger. Some updating systems require that the processing of a transaction be entirely separate from the creation of a new record. That is, you cannot enter both the new record and the first transaction to it at the time that you first create it.

3. Date of the most recent master files that can be used

After the system has been in operation for a year, and the secretary is on vacation, it is convenient to know which file is the one to update. Then again, even if the secretary isn't on vacation, it might be handy to rely on something other than one person's memory. After all, the secretary may run 3 different systems on 3 different days during the week.

4. Which system date, if any, is to be entered

Besides the current files, there are at least two generations of backup files in existence. Confusion could be very close if no written date index exists.

Perhaps the system uses the current date. Then again, perhaps the user didn't complete everything the day before, and those transactions must go under yesterday's date. The current date is adequate 99 times out of 100, but who knows? Perhaps the package won't handle leap years—it's been known to happen.

5. **Things to have ready before entering the main phase**

Soft-sectored disks are *initialized*, set up, by software. If the program you are running requires a blank, initialized disk and you don't have one available, you must terminate the current job, run the initializing routine, reload your program, and return to where you left off.

Small computers do not always have the capacity to put one job on hold while you do another. In order to save time, frustration, and additional cause for error, it is advisable to have ready things that will be needed during the course of running a job. (See Figure 15.)

6. **How to take backup**

It is important to be able to recreate your current business records in case something should happen to them. *Backup* is a term used to mean a complete copy of your most recently updated records which is stored in a safe place. This is usually done by some method of rotating past and present copies.

The grandparent method creates an original. That original is then updated and completely copied to a separate storage medium. (Many users make two copies and store one off the premises.) This current version is then the child of the original version called the parent. The process continues one more time, so that the parent becomes the grandparent, the child becomes the parent, and the original grandparent is retired and used to become the current child (see Figure 16). However, some users like to keep backup to the great-grandparent.

The calendar method sets up a separate duplicate storage media

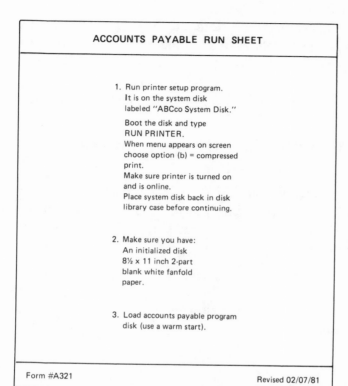

Figure 15

for certain cycles of time. It may be a weekly or monthly cycle. With a weekly cycle of 5 working days, you would have 6 separate storage media marked Monday, Tuesday, and so on. At the end of each day, you would copy your current version onto the storage medium for that day. The advantages of this version are that you always know which backup is which and you are never more than one step away from being current. In the example in Figure 17, there is one parent data medium, for a total of 6 different storage media. Disks have been used in this illustration; however, the principle remains the same regardless of the technology.

Whichever method you use, you have to keep a file of the transactions that brought about the changes to your record. In a small business system, there are usually hard copy records stored in a safe place. Sophisticated computer systems often keep track

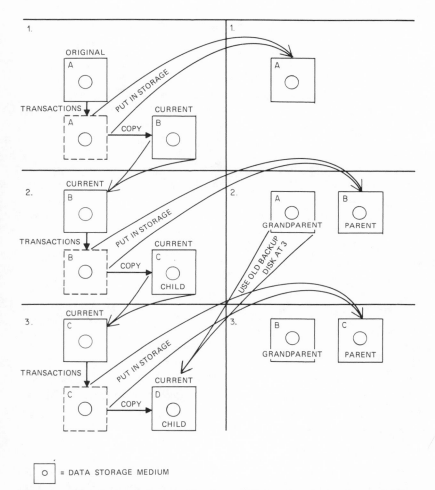

Figure 16 Generational Backup Method: Grandparent—Parent—Child.

of these changes in a separate electronic file called a *transaction log*. Depending on the sophistication of the system and the amount of information, the transaction log may range from minutes to hours.

7. When to take backup

A rule of thumb is to take backup when changes to the file represent 15 to 20 minutes of a person's time. If you edited the

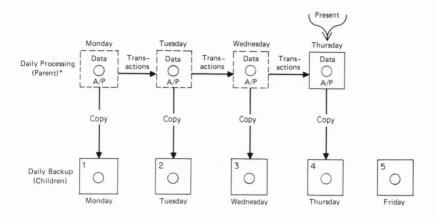

*Dotted disks indicate passage of parent medium.

Figure 17 Calendar Backup Method.

master file and changed 15 records, you should back up your new file.

You must take backup at the completion of a job if it changed any record values and a transaction log was not automatically generated. Backup is designed to protect your information base and give you the ability to recreate it quickly if it is damaged. You may run a job which requires no input from you, but which changes certain field values in a file. Later on, that file will be used for another job. You never want to be more than one cycle of activity away from a current set of information.

8. Where to store backup

The purpose of backup is to have in existence a complete set of your information that is protected from destruction, accidental or otherwise.

Backup information must be kept physically separate and distinct from the working set. At the very least, keep backup on a separate shelf, not in the same box. If possible, keep your backup in a separate room.

Some of the possible causes of damage to your data base are:

a. Entering incorrect information, innocently or on purpose
b. Physical destruction of the storage medium, innocently or on purpose

Actions which can lead to physical destruction of an off-line storage medium include:

a. Dropping the device
b. Dropping things on the device, such as soda pop, coffee, cigarette ash, and so on
c. Fire on the premises
d. Theft by an irate employee

9. Exiting the system gracefully

When a job is completed, the items which were used should be put back in their place. Software systems open and close files and move information from one place to another, and it is best to close all files before leaving the system. It is always possible to exit a system by physically turning off the computer, but this can lead to lost transactions and incomplete updates. There is usually an exit option available in a well-designed system, and it should be utilized.

10. Order of powering down the equipment

Powering down the hardware in the incorrect order can lead to loss of data. If there is a necessary sequence, it should be documented in the work and procedures manual and also on the individual hardware pieces within the system.

Types of Files: What do I want to do to my data?

Files, manual or electronic, exist to provide some form of modular update capability. Manually, we use paper as the initial record base and then organize our system around the storage of the individual paper records. These paper records may be 3 × 5 index cards, 8½ ×

11 sheets of paper, or larger sheets of paper. When setting up a manual filing system, we try to take into account how to best organize the files for easy use. The end user of a computer system has the same concern.

ELECTRONIC FILES

The major concern is the amount of access available to the user. Hardware and software limitations are to be expected, but sometimes software designers impose limitations that are not in the user's best interest.

Compatibility refers to the ability of different systems to exchange data. An accounting system that utilizes a totally unique file structure and does not allow the user program access to the file effectively limits the file information to the accounting system. You may want to use some of that information in a word processing system. You may want to put your system online to a larger computer. If you cannot get to the data files, then you cannot use those files in other programs. Compatibility is not always a necessity, but it can be necessary for future growth.

Record Retention: How long before I can throw it out?

In addition to legal and tax requirements for record retention, there is an electronic consideration. Basically, the questions are:

1. What to keep?

2. When to destroy?

The minimum requirement for record retention is the least amount of information necessary to recreate the current data base. This might be satisfied by the grandparent system of backup. If the current file is the child, then you should have the previous generation (parent) and the generation previous to that (grandparent) in existence at all times. It is also necessary to keep the associated physical change records for those generations. Otherwise, you would have no means of moving up from the previous generation to the offspring.

Another consideration with record retention is, "who authorizes the destruction?" Guidelines concerning what is to be destroyed should be documented. At or before the time that action takes place, a manager should sign off on the documents.

THINGS TO GUARD AGAINST

Computer systems do not display their data bases physically at all times. Also, they do not physically indicate changes. With a manual record-keeping system, it is possible to see if a column is blank or even if data has been scratched out, erased, and replaced. It is not as easy to look through a computer system.

Data Checking: Am I sure that the system is getting reasonable input?

The process of verifying data ranges from double-checking input to providing parameters at the time of input. If 50 records a day are being edited and you assume a 95 percent success rate, then at least 2 records a day will be incorrect. That's a minimum of 40 a month. Built in checks include:

1. Defining data boundaries. Only numeric information is accepted by some fields. Range limits are present; inventory numbers, for example, must be between 1000 and 10,000. Certain running totals are kept and periodically checked.

2. Entering the same data a second time as a verify mode (only used in systems where data input is intensive).

Physical Data Loss: Have I guarded against accidents?

It is the nature of electronic equipment to be prey to electronic ills. Line fluctuations can cause misreads and miswrites. Variance in the speed of disk drives can cause I/O errors. Static electricity generated by the operator can affect computer memory. The solutions are to determine the manufacturer's power and installation requirements and to provide for a physical maintenance schedule on necessary hardware. At worst, the replacement cost of a small disk drive is less than the replacement cost of 6 month's work.

Hardware is also prey to accidents. Because small computers and their associated devices are so small, people tend to leave them lying around. Cigarette smoke, drinks, food, the pressure of a person leaning on a disk can all disrupt stored data. Extremes of temperature can affect equipment and storage media. External magnetic storage cannot be folded, spindled, or stapled.

It is always a good idea to read the packaging for tips on how to handle the contents. Best of all, post a list of physical restrictions near the hardware for the day that you have someone standing in for a regular employee.

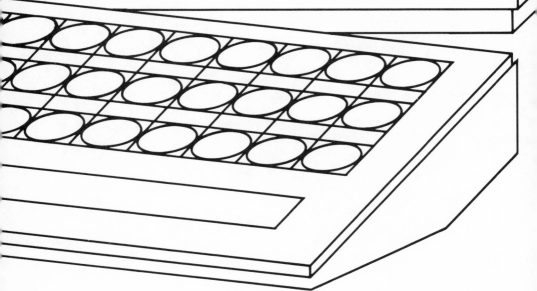

8 WHAT DOES IT ALL COST?

8 WHAT DOES IT ALL COST?

Determine the cost of the computer. Then determine the cost of the computer system in use.

I. TAKING A LONG, HARD LOOK AT WHAT IS IN-
VOLVED

II. START-UP COST
1. Machine Size: What initial price constrictions do I have?
2. Small User: Do I require individual, limited application functions?
3. Medium User: Do a number of different people utilize the system?

4. Large User: Are time and presentation of the essence?

III. LONG-TERM COST
1. Programs or Packages: Is there an existing package that meets my application needs in the way I want?
2. System Costs: Have I budgeted for personnel, space, supplies, and additional business expenses?
3. Types of Vendors: Why am I buying from the place I'm buying from?

TAKING A LONG, HARD LOOK AT WHAT IS INVOLVED

The overestimated side of computers is what computers can do, and the most underestimated side is what they cost. Computers come in many different shapes, sizes, and flavors, like airplanes. A passenger-carrying jet and a single-engine plane both fly, but you don't expect a single-engine plane to carry 200-plus passengers. On the other hand, a jet has difficulty landing in a small field. What you want from a plane determines the choice.

For a lot of money, you can fly first class from Los Angeles to London whenever you want without much prebooking. For little money, you can fly from Los Angeles to London with no class, at a time convenient to the airline with a fair bit of preplanning. Computers are the same way. The thrust of this chapter is to show the cost of computers and computing in terms of money and time. Too often, the cost of time is ignored in dealing with small computers. More money will not always buy more time.

The power of a computer lies in the software that exists for it. Qualified, trained software authors (programmers) are extremely scarce. And the proliferation of different technological solutions makes it extremely unlikely that the situation will change. It is not hopeless; rather, like everything else, the computer world is a trade-off.

Hardware costs are a small part of setting up and using a computerized system. In fact, it is currently possible to put together a system with floppy disks, printer, CPU, keyboard, screen, and a number of software packages for under $3000. The cost is in utilizing the system to give you what you want when you want it.

START-UP COST

Because of the rapid development of hardware technology, it is difficult to say what constitutes a small computer, a medium computer, or a large computer. At one time, computers were described according to the size of their memory, which was related to their physical size. Large computers were called mainframes, medium computers were called minis, and small computers were called micros.

Machine Size: What initial price constrictions do I have?

From the point of view of systems analysis, a more realistic example is the amount of money spent on hardware (see Figure 18).

Small User: Do I require individual, limited application functions?

UP TO $5000

Computer systems in this price range are usually excellent tools for the individual user. They provide the user with individual spread sheet analysis, electronic filing, and limited word processing capabilities. The business (accounting) functions are of the small, under-10-person business variety. Most of the software will require that you adapt to it.

This equipment can be used as part of a larger computer system. However, then it acts as a terminal in a network and is a $5000 terminal per work station, not a $5000, computer system.

Medium User: Do a number of different people utilize the system?

$5000 TO $15,000

These machines are professional systems for the small business. They have all the individual user capabilities with certain added features.

	Up to $5000	$5000 to $15,000	$15,000 on up
Uses	1. Individual use tool 2. Limited business	1. Work station 2. Single use, small business	1. Work station 2. Multiuse
Packages Available	1. Many; often rigid in format 2. Adapt business to package	1. Vast number 2. Aimed at small business market	1. Many 2. Often have programs written for specific needs

Figure 18 Machine Size by Cost.

This means that it is easier to do more sophisticated things. The business functions are more professional and easier to use.

In this price range, computer systems are often dedicated to a particular function for a specific business. You might, for example, purchase a system specifically for the accounting needs of a physician's practice, or a system may be aimed squarely at the word processing needs of legal firm.

Large User: Are time and presentation of the essence?

$15,000 AND UP

These machines are faster and can do more things at once. Many fine packages exist for many different markets. A business invests in this type of system for the same reason that you buy a first-class ticket on a passenger plane: you will get where you want to go quickly, safely, and comfortably. Also, you will not have to know how to fly an airplane.

LONG-TERM COST

Over the operating life of your system, the least expensive item will be the computer and the most expensive will be personnel. The difference between a $4000 computer and a $5000 computer may be an additional row of keys at the terminal. But those extra keys mean a more relaxed, happier operator working at 90 percent efficiency, rather than 75 percent.

With small computers, you do not have to worry about the expense of reinforcing the floor or providing special environments. You do have to worry about the effect it will have on you and your employees. Things like keyboard touch, screen color, and ambient light reflection are the difference between a professional computer system that will be used and one that gathers dust.

Because small computers are not hidden away from the work force, it is important that they blend into or complement their surroundings. When purchasing computer furniture, make sure that it is well-designed, functionally and aesthetically. Computer furniture in a business office, for example, should not have sharp corners that can injure passing employees.

Programs or Packages: Is there an existing package that meets my application needs in the way I want?

Regardless of hardware cost, virtually all computer systems are programmable. However, keep in mind that a full-time programmer on a large computer is considered a trainee for at least 6 months. Then remember that a small computer is just about as programmable as a large one.

When it comes to writing programs, the industry standard is 25 lines of assembly language code a day. And regardless of what the salesperson tells you, the same numbers are probably true for all programming languages. What a higher level language buys you is mainly shorter learning time. Those 25 lines represent design, coding, debugging, and documentation, and one application program, such as accounts payable, is approximately 1000 lines of code.

It is the experience of the professionals involved in the computer industry that most estimates of programming time fall short. This is probably true of the chart in Figure 19. If you can live with the restrictions of packaged programs, the time you will save can be enormous.

A good, professional business package should guide the user on the computer. A rule of thumb for business packages: the more you spend on them, the less you have to figure out. With a sophisticated, user-friendly (that's what costs money) package, a person can sit down at a computer and be utilizing it in 1 to 5 hours. Of course, learning to utilize a package is only one part; data entry still has to take place for most systems to operate.

System Costs: Have I budgeted for personnel, space, supplies, and additional business expenses?

Computer operation of even the friendliest system requires an individual with secretarial abilities. Whatever you expect of a good secretary, the computer expects of the operator. The ability to read, follow instructions, utilize initiative, be neat, pay attention to details, and be

Languages and utilities	For beginner to learn properly	To write a simple general personal ledger	To write a simple business general ledger	To write a sophisticated accounting ledger
BASIC COBOL	25 to 100 hours	100 to 300 hours	200 to 400 hours	600 to 1200 hours
FORTRAN PLI PASCAL	Around 75 hours	Around 300 hours	Around 400 hours	Around 1000 hours
Programming utilities. Data base managers with query languages	25 to 100 hours	50 to 200 hours	100 to 250 hours	700 hours
Electronic filing utilities with report generation	10 to 20 hours	25 to 50 hours (more of a filing system)	Not possible	Not possible

Figure 19   Programming Time.

patient is essential. You can assume that whatever it costs in your area of the country to purchase these attributes on an hourly basis will be the hourly operating cost of your computer. The cost of operating the system will also include the time of any other involved individuals. These range from data entry personnel to technical advisors.

SPACE

A computer system takes up space. If it takes up the area of one desk, that is the space cost. Associated supplies have to be stored somewhere. Many businesses keep their backup disks in a safety deposit box at the bank. If you don't have one, this is an additional, although small, expense.

SUPPLIES

If you are using floppy disks for storage, you can expect to end up with anywhere from 50 to 100 floppy disks, and you should plan on replacing frequently used data disks every 6 months. Compared to the value of your business data, disks are inexpensive.

The best advice on disks is to buy the best, whatever the cost. Call up a software publisher and ask to speak to one of the programmers. A programmer knows the frustration of working with bad disks. A good disk is one that accepts and gives up data easily without errors. A bad disk is one that has lots of read-write errors and hangs up the processing.

Other necessary supplies include paper, which is inexpensive and can be purchased from any paper supplier, and print ribbons, which are often of a special type. Check the manual that comes with the printer to see which type you will need.

Types of Vendors: Why am I buying
from the place I'm buying from?

Small computers are marketed in every way imaginable. The guiding principle in purchasing your equipment should be: what will it cost me over the period of a year?

DEALERS

Some computer manufacturers give special preference to their registered dealers. Usually, this means that they have access to hardware supplies on a timely basis. Not all dealers are specialists in the equipment they sell. Often, a retailer attains a dealership by selling a set number of machines per month. A good dealer will know of professionals in the area whom you can hire for specialized needs.

Advantages.   Dealers are in direct contact with the hardware manufacturers. They can often provide very competitive prices. If they specialize in one or two manufacturers, they may be knowledgeable about the equipment.

Disadvantages.   Dealers are in the business of selling computers and cannot always give individual customers the attention they need. They may be limited in the type of hardware they carry, and dealers often sell packaged application programs as a convenience. This means that they cannot make the purchaser aware of other possibilities.

SYSTEM HOUSES

A system house is a company that addresses itself to a particular market and sells complete solutions for that market. They will provide preanalysis, hardware, software, and training for a fee. Some system houses are registered dealers. Others buy the equipment from wholesalers and resell it.

Advantages.   System houses provide a complete package. They should know both the hardware and the software in some detail. They should make it their business to know your business and come to you. You will receive a degree of individual attention.

Disadvantages.   The initial cost is higher. They may not be willing to provide extensive changes outside of their existing applications. They are usually locally oriented.

THE COMPUTER STORE

These are retail establishments specializing in computers. They usually carry a large variety of hardware and software and can provide some technical assistance. But basically shopping in a computer store is like shopping in a hi-fi store.

Advantages.   A wide selection and a chance to try out some equipment before you purchase. Many stores are part of a nationwide chain. This can be helpful if you have many different business locations. It also means that they can get certain equipment when other smaller retailers have run out.

Disadvantages.   Most computer salespeople have to make sales in order to survive. Their primary interest is in selling hardware. You cannot always expect individual attention.

MAIL ORDER

This ranges from stores and dealers who sell their products through the mail to individuals who act as purchasing agents. Mail order is usually cheaper. Probably the major difference between mail order and on-site purchasing is that you will receive equipment that has not been assembled and tested since it left the factory. A good computer store, dealer, or software house will set up and run a system before it is sold.

Advantages.   Savings on purchase price. On some items, this can be as much as 35 percent or more.

Disadvantages.   You need to know what you are buying and be able to set it up yourself. It can be much more time consuming in that you will have to burn in the equipment yourself. To *burn in* the equipment means to leave the computer on for about 30 hours while it does some test program. The idea is to force those electronic circuits that are weak to fail before you go into production.

CONSULTANTS

These are individuals whom you hire for their experience. Consultants may act for you in purchasing equipment, or they may be retained to design software or provide training. A consultant is hired for two main reasons:

1. To get you exactly what you want.

2. To advise you about alternatives if number 1 is not possible.

The best time to hire a consultant is before you begin a project. Your local computer store will usually know of individuals who are consulting on a freelance basis. You can also call local schools and colleges and inquire if faculty members consult or can recommend one of their students. You should be interested in the department of business studies first, computer science second.

Hiring a consultant is much the same as hiring a lawyer; you hope to get sound advice, but there is no guarantee that you will win your particular case. Any reputable consultant will provide you with references. Having done that, see how well the consultant understands you and how well you understand the consultant.

Consultants are paid in numerous ways, from an hourly to a daily to a per project basis. Hourly rates for professional consultants are high and are not worthwhile unless you are a capable project manager. There are ways to save on consulting costs. However, the risk you take is proportionally higher.

Offer to trade with the consultant for part of the fee. You can offer computer time and even help in selling additional systems along the lines the consultant is developing for you.

In dealing with a consultant, set up cutoff points at which either one of you can bail out.

Some things a consultant cannot do:

1. Make up for the lack of adequate budgeting.

2. Computerize your business overnight.

3. Give you everything you want all the time.

Advantages.   A consultant works for you and may save you a great deal of time and money over the long haul.

Disadvantages.   High initial cost.

SERVICE CONTRACTS

These are yearly contracts to take care of your hardware. The industry standard is that about 10 percent of your hardware cost will be your annual fee. A service contract is like car insurance, when the machine breaks down, the repair bills are covered. However, there are certain things to keep in mind concerning service contracts and the way small computer manufacturers are set up.

Some, but not all, service contracts specify that a service person will come to your site and fix the machine. Many service contracts provide for the pickup and delivery of the component. Either the malfunctioning component will be replaced then and there, or your component will be returned in working order within 24 to 72 hours.

Do you need a service contract? If you need continuous operation, the answer is an unqualified yes. If you can live with your system being down for a couple of days, the answer is maybe. To determine the answer, you have to consider what requires servicing.

A computer can be seen as made up of two types of equipment, electronic and mechanical. Once a computer has been up and running for a few months, the chances of an electronic component failing are fairly slim. The chances of a mechanical component failing are much greater.

Computer hardware, at least the mechanical pieces, are expected to last about a year between failures and, of course, the more mechanical peripherals you have, the more chance of failure at separate times.

Printers and disk drives are the pieces that need the most attention. Sometimes it can be quicker and less expensive to put the equipment in the back of your car and drive over to the service drop. Or, you may wish to send it yourself by commercial carrier to the local service depot and pay the individual rate.

Advantages.   Peace of mind and less personal involvement.

Disadvantages.   A high cost that may not be justifiable.

INSURANCE

Small computers are very portable. It is a good idea to budget for both theft and destruction insurance.

COMMUNICATION COSTS

If you have a system that utilizes a telephone or other commercial communication channels, there will be an additional monthly charge for that service.

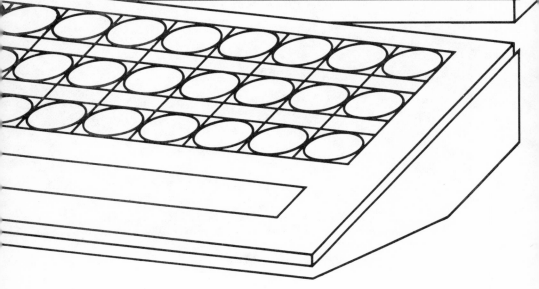

9 IMPLEMEN-TATION

9 IMPLEMENTATION

Have an orderly sequence of steps to transfer your business from its current system to the computer system.

I. CHECK LIST FOR CONTROLLING THE CHANGE-OVER
1. The Need for a Computer: Why do you and your employees want a computer?
2. Budget: How much are you going to spend over the period of a year?
3. Managing the Job: Who will oversee the project?
4. Preanalysis: Are my business needs understood?
5. Revision: In light of what I have learned so far, what changes do I have to make to my original expectations?

6. Priorities: What do I want now and what can wait?
7. Gantt Chart: Have I assigned enough time for training and data entry?
8. Work and Procedures: Who is expected to do what?
9. Setting Up the Data Base: Do I have all the input available to start putting it into the computer?
10. Parallel Testing: Have I taken into account that I will be running the old and new systems concurrently?
11. Catch-Up Days: Have I allowed enough time for things to go wrong and still be on schedule?

CHECK LIST FOR CONTROLLING THE CHANGEOVER

Installing a new computer is like falling in love. At the very beginning, you know everything is perfect and it is a match made in heaven. Just before the engagement, you are slightly panicked, wondering what you are getting into. Then, the day of the marriage is exciting, nerve-wracking, and one you will always remember. During the honeymoon period, certain idiosyncracies become apparent, but love makes them adorable. Then, you settle down into the give and take of married life. How well the marriage survives the give and take depends on the expectations of the parties involved.

Long engagements may not always be in style for marriages, but they are definitely always in style for computer systems. The installation of a new computer system commits your business to the union. Therefore, the value of the system is not the cost of the hardware, software, and operation, rather, it is the value of the business itself. One step at a time is the way to go.

The Need for a Computer: Why do you and your employees want a computer?

Before you do anything else, make a list of the answers to this question. Somewhere in that list should be the answer, "because everyone else has one." More computers, large and small, have been bought for this reason than any other. If you don't admit to this desire at the start, it will get in the way time and time again. It will influence your choices by justifying the purchase regardless of any other reasons. By acknowledging this desire, you can weigh it along with the other factors you will list.

The following are some common justifications for buying a small computer.

It will save time. Not really true. It is the overall system that should save time by utilizing the correct computer with the proper programs.

It is more efficient. Sometimes it is; sometimes it is not. It depends on what you are doing. Sometimes a box of index cards can be more efficient.

It will improve the business. If the business is dying, a computer will do nothing but hasten the death. If the business is alive, it can be an enormous aid to expansion.

It will free me or my employee to do other things. Maybe, but someone has to mind the baby. When the computer is used as a personal tool, it can save enormous amounts of time. When the computer is used as a clerk to do repetitive work, it needs to be cared for. From the point of view of the employee, the quality of work is changed. It is more fun to run a computer than to sort files.

When you make up your list, be specific. Think in terms of accounting, word processing, management information, and the like. At the beginning stage, don't talk to anyone outside of your business. You are trying to determine what you want, not what others think you need.

Budget: How much are you going to spend over the period of a year?

Having made out your wish list, choose an amount of money you are prepared to spend over a year to get those wishes. Know what you can afford and assign a range. Be aware of your absolute maximum amount. Again, do this before you speak to salespeople, consultants, or other interested parties.

Now double your maximum amount. This will give you a rough feel for what a new system may cost. That amount will be spent in cold cash or in time. Prepare yourself.

Managing the Job: Who will oversee the project?

Someone in your organization must oversee the activity of the computerization. A consultant or software house can do the majority of the work, but someone in your business must make the decisions. This means they must become acquainted with what is important in judging a new system.

Preanalysis: Are my business needs understood?

Using your wish list and your rough budget as parameters, have someone do the preliminary analysis. In managing this task, you would like to see the following activities:

1. An analysis of your company—Chapter 2

2. A look at your environment—Chapter 6

3. A rough budget—Chapter 8

Revision: In light of what I have learned so far, what changes do I have to make to my original expectations?

The results of the preanalysis should be weighed against your original desires for a computer. This is often a good place to bail out. The cost of the equipment may be too high. It may be that the system is not really going to buy you anything. Your priorities may be mixed up; as much as you need a computer, you really need to improve sales, number of clients serviced, or whatever first.

Priorities: What do I want now and what can wait?

It always takes longer than you would like, and it definitely takes longer than anyone estimates. Figure out what is the most important thing that you want the computer to do first, second, third, and so on. It is only by determining your priorities that you can create a Gantt chart.

Gantt Chart: Have I assigned enough time for training and data entry?

This is a simple time chart. It is invaluable for scheduling the introduction of a new system. It is also helpful in keeping track of the project.

Gantt charts usually run horizontally. They can be in either linear or strip format, and they are broken down into reasonable time units. A chart of this type is used in Chapter 11.

A Gantt chart is only effective when it displays all the time-bound variables involved in implementation. Some of these variables are:

Setup time.   Wires may have to be run; hardware may have to be configured; and software may have to be configured. (See Figure 20.)

Training time.   The "push one button and it goes" machine does not exist. Employees must be shown how to create backup, what to do when things go wrong, and all the associated details of operating the

Word processor	0 to 2 hours	It can create new letter/report right away. Formatting the material to be printed can take some time.
Electronic spread sheet	1 to 25 hours	The minimum time is to set up your formulas and then enter first set of data. The maximum time depends on the size and complexity of your spread sheet. With these types of packages you usually set up the formulas yourself. It is possible to buy additional packages that are the templates (formulas) and enter data.
Off-the-shelf accounting package (general ledger)	5 to 25 hours	All require that you assign some values to the system, for example your journal headings. Also you have to enter some data records, enough to completely test the system.
Electronic filing systems	1 to 10 hours	You have to lay out record and report formats.
Relational data base	15 minutes to 10+ hours	The minimum time is to set up record and use report generator; open-ended if you decide to program with the query language.
Hierarchical data base	days+	Very complicated to set up.

Figure 20   Chart of Setup Times. Assumes knowledge of use of software.

hardware. Someone has to show you how to set the top of the page indicator for your printer.

Date entry time.   If you are going to get anything out of the system, you must put it all in to begin with. An accounts receivable system that keeps track of 1000 customers has to have them on file somewhere.

You may have to put this chart together yourself, but it is worth the effort. The place to get the estimates of how long these three variables will take is from another user. You should be able to get the name of another purchaser from your supplier. Also, try contacting computer clubs in your area. There is usually a business-oriented section of the club. If you are having a system written from scratch, remember the industry average is approximately 40 days per application program, and a number of programs may make up the entire system.

Work and Procedures: Who is expected to do what?

Your new system will require that certain things be done in a certain way. You need to know the methods and procedures of the system. Chapter 10 of this book details the documentation of this section. There are two areas that you need to know for the daily operation of your system:

1. The order of operation—a run chart

2. Access to information

RUN CHART

This is nothing more than a diagram of what must be done in what order. They should be complete and include all operational steps. The chart should detail:

1. How to get into the system

2. What is required by the software, i.e., data input, blank disks, and 8½-inch paper.

3. A list of possible error messages

4. What to do when an error message is received

5. How to quit the system

ACCESS TO INFORMATION

Have a list of (1) where the manuals are located and (2) whom to call in an emergency with the hardware or software. Keep track of all your manuals and all the documentation that comes with your system. At some point in time, having the manual available will save someone hours of work.

Setting Up the Data Base: Do I have all the input available to start putting it into the computer?

Once you have a Gantt chart in front of you, you will know what to expect. If your new system requires data input to set it up, try to make sure that the data will be available. This step is often overlooked, and enormous amounts of time are wasted.

A major advantage to having real data available for computer entry is that it facilitates the training period. People learn faster when using actual, sensible material, as compared to artificial test data. A second benefit is that you will begin to see how well the new system handles your data. You can use this period as a tuning-up time.

Parallel Testing: Have I taken into account that I will be running the old and new systems concurrently?

When everything is in place and you have tested all aspects of the system, you are ready to do parallel testing.

Parallel testing means using the same live data in the new system as you are using in the existing system. You should run parallel for at least 3 months before switching your business to the new system, and make sure the results compare exactly.

This principle is especially critical when your new system involves storage, data manipulation, and retrieval. Accounting systems of all types are particularly prone to showing up with little bugs only after you have run them for a while.

Catch-Up Days: Have I allowed enough time for things to go wrong and still be on schedule?

In any system that you implement, allow time for things to not be on time. With new computer systems, one catch-up day in four is a reasonable estimate. Even if you are installing a so-called turn-key system with off-the-shelf packages, include these catch-up days.

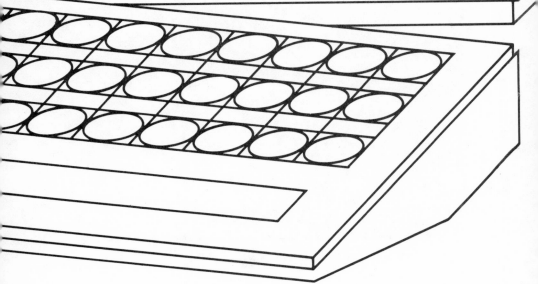
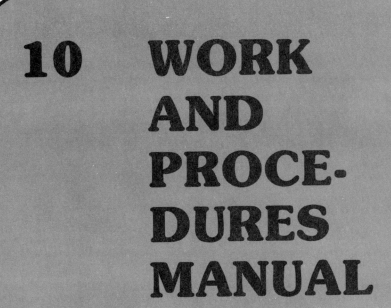

10 WORK AND PROCE-DURES MANUAL

10 WORK AND PROCEDURES MANUAL

Provide clear, concise references for operating your computer system. Create it out of your research into the installation of your new system.

I. GETTING IT DOWN ON PAPER

II. SETTING UP THE MANUAL
1. Table of Contents: Have I divided by manual into appropriate sections?
2. Record Keeping: Have I kept track of each step since I decided to consider a computer?
3. Starting and Stopping the System: Do I know how and in what order to turn everything on and off?
4. Setting Up: Have I documented how to load paper, disks, and other media?
5. Electronic File Names: What are the rules governing the creation of names?
6. Operating System Limitations: Am I clear as to why this operating system is being used?
7. Application Program Limitations: Have I listed the constraints each program imposes?
8. Housekeeping: Have I documented the necessary routines that keep things moving along?

9. Physical Labels: Have I specified enough information to adequately describe individual storage mediums?
10. Application Synopsis: Do I have brief descriptions of
    what each application does?
11. Run Sheets: Have I laid out the sequence of steps
    necessary to operate a particular program?
12. I/O Samples: Have I included all input and output
    samples with each program?
13. Distribution: Is it clear as to who gets what?
14. Electronic File Catalog: Am I keeping track of what
    data I am putting in what files?
15. Glossary: Do I know what everything means?
16. Error Messages: Is it clear what the system is
    communicating?
17. Emergency Procedures: Have I covered myself?
18. User Log: Do I want to keep a diary of system
    activity?

GETTING IT DOWN ON PAPER

The work and procedures manual is the book of instructions for your computer system. It is not always easy to set up and maintain, as people tend to see it as just another chore. However, the manual is worth the effort the first time your regular computer operator is home sick and a temporary person has to run the invoices.

A work and procedures manual is both a reference volume and a diary. It can be created as you design or install a new system, or you can set it up during the parallel testing phase. The manual should be easily accessible, and it should be a copy of the original, which is stored in a safe place. A good manual will contain information on operating procedures, operating conventions, and reference material. Sometimes a separate operations log detailing what was actually run is kept with it.

The purpose of the manual is to be an easy and ready reference; therefore, entries should be brief and clear. If further elaboration is required, reference should be made to the specific literature in your master library. Computer systems spawn printed matter at the same rate as fans boo an umpire. Every piece of equipment, every piece of software, will come with its own manual, sheet of instructions, or reference card. You don't have to read them all, but they must all be kept together in an accessible place.

The other library you will have to reference is your program library. Regardless of your storage system, the original of your programs will be kept on different floppy disks. These disks must be kept somewhere in some order. They too will be referenced by your work and procedures manual.

SETTING UP THE MANUAL

The work and procedures manual should be a three-ring binder that is physically easy to handle and can lay flat when open to any page. Various types of inexpensive plastic page holders are available at stationery stores. They are excellent for holding pages or samples of reference material.

The outside of the manual should be clearly labeled with a title and where it is to be kept. Plan for the time your bookkeeper's son comes to the office and moves the manual.

Pages in the manual should be numbered at the top. Put the date of creation at the bottom. You are sure to make revisions, and it helps to know that you have the latest version. Separate the sections by tabbed dividers.

SOME LAYOUT NOTES

Place run sheets and I/O samples on facing pages to make life easier for the operator. You also may want to break down your application programs by section—all inventory in one, payroll programs in another, and so on. Emergency procedures should be in a section by themselves at the end for quick and easy reference.

Table of Contents: Have I divided my manual into appropriate sections?

A sample table of contents would include most of the following:

1. How to start and stop the equipment

2. How to set up individual equipment

3. Conventions for electronic file names

4. Operating system limitations

5. Application program limitations

6. Housekeeping procedures

7. Conventions for storage labels

8. Application synopsis

9. Run sheets

10. I/O samples

11. Distribution chart

12. Electronic file catalog

13. Glossary of terms

14. Error messages

15. Emergency procedures

Not all of these have to be in separate sections. They should, however, be referenced separately. You may prefer to divide your book up into larger units:

1. The equipment
   a. Starting, stopping, and setting-up procedures
   b. Conventions for storage labels
   c. Conventions for electronic file names
   d. Operating system limitations
   e. Catalog of all electronic files
   f. Housekeeping procedures

2. Application programs
   a. Program limitations
   b. Application synopsis
   c. Distribution chart
   d. Run sheets, I/O samples on facing pages
   e. Error messages

3. Emergency procedures

4. Glossary

Record Keeping: Have I kept track of each
step since I decided to consider a computer?

An easy way to set up this manual is to build it as you go along. The day you decide to seriously consider a new system is the day to set aside a three-ring binder with this title and then divide it into sections to be filled in later.

Information gathered during the design of the system will satisfy many of the sections of this manual. The order might be as follows:

1. **Application program limitations**

You will begin to find this out in your preliminary analysis. After all, if the accountant tells you that it is possible to get by with six-digit accuracy, this is one of the potential limitations.

2. **Application synopsis**

Before you even buy anything, you should have most of this. The rule is to buy software that meets your requirements and hardware that meets the software requirements. This synopsis represents your requirements.

3. **I/O samples and distribution chart**

These will turn up as you do the application synopsis. They are part of the research to determine your needs.

4. **Glossary of terms**

This will grow out of the previous steps. If you have set up your manual, you can enter specific definitions as they come up.

5. **Emergency procedures**

You should determine early on in your analysis what to do when things go wrong. This information is part of your buying decision.

6. **Operating system limitations**

There are a number of operating systems available. Many are look-alikes and can operate in place of one another, but there are differences. Insist on an answer. This is the last of the decisions that commit you, so document it now before you buy.

7. **Housekeeping procedures**

By now, you have decided what to purchase, so this is the place to list the housekeeping routines.

8. **Starting, stopping, and setting up equipment**

You should set this section up during the initial phase of installing the equipment.

9. **Error messages**

This section will grow out of the previous section. When your equipment is first set up and you are practicing with it, make some intentional errors, then record the results.

10. **File names and storage labeling**

Now that you've made a few intentional errors and have seen that the equipment hasn't gone up in smoke, you will want to begin doing some testing. This is the point to set up file names and storage labels. Do it now before confusion grows.

11. **Electronic file catalog**

Now that you're beginning to run serious tests, you need to keep track of your files. This will help you evaluate your tests and be ready for running applications.

12. **Run sheets**

The last series of tests before you begin to run parallel tests will be a complete run through of the application. Document them and your records will be complete.

Starting and Stopping the System: Do I know how and in what order to turn everything on and off?

This is where you detail how to turn every piece of equipment on and off. If some equipment has hard-to-find switches, this is the place to explain where they are.

Some computer systems require that equipment be turned on and off in a certain order. Detail that order here. Also, label the individual equipment with these details.

Setting Up: Have I documented how
to load paper, disks, and other media?

Printers provide the most possibilities for getting things slightly wrong. Here you should detail how to set up the top of the form indicator, how to set vertical tabs if they exist, and how to set up any other features your programs may require. Copy the relevant pages in the printer manual that explain these functions. Copy the illustrations of how to load different types of paper. Show how to change the ribbon and indicate where supplies are found.

This is the section where you should talk about the care and handling of floppy disks and any other sensitive storage mediums.

Tell the reader what to do if supplies run out. Who orders the floppy disks? What number do they call? Do you require single-sided, double-sided, double-density, or other types of disks? Spell out details.

Electronic File Names: What are the
rules governing the creation of names?

In some of your application programs, you will be saving data in files that you create and name. There may be length and character limitations to the name. Also, you may want all accounting file names to start with an "A." Or, you may want a word processing name to indicate by some convention if it is a letter, report, or boiler plate paragraph. There may be a limit to the number of names you can store in a disk directory, so that even if a disk is not full, you won't be able to write any more information on it. All this and anything else your system requires of file names go in this section.

Operating System Limitations: Am I clear
as to why this operating system is being used?

There may be a limit to the number of terminals you can use at one time. Terminal response time can drop off dramatically with the addition of just one terminal over the best operating limit.

Certain default file names are acceptable, others are not. You should indicate which ones you are using.

Application Program Limitations: Have I listed
the constraints each program imposes?

Here you would indicate the maximum number of records that can be
stored. There may be a limitation on the number of customer or client
records that can be placed on each storage medium.

Certain word processing programs have an optimum file size. Some
have limitations on the types of characters you can enter. There may
be a limitation on the amount of information you can cut and paste
internally. A financial program may only be accurate to 10 places. This
is the place to spell it out.

Housekeeping: Have I documented the necessary
routines that keep things moving along?

It may be necessary to format your blank disks electronically before
they can be used by the system. Explain the procedure in simple steps.
Give examples of how to copy whole disks, groups of files, or
individual files, and explain your backup procedures from start to
finish. Show how to get information from the computer regarding its
own status. There are built-in system commands, for example, which
determine how much useable space is left on a disk.

Physical Labels: Have I specified enough information
to adequately describe individual storage media?

When you use a number of floppy disks or other removable storage
media, explain the required minimum amount of information that goes
on a physically attached label. This usually consists of the following:

- The name of the program that created it.

- The date it was created.

- What's on it—generally.

- The type of disk—some programs create separate disks to handle a
  data base. You may need a data disk and a system disk for the
  program to operate.

- Whether it is a current or a backup disk.

- The initials of the person who created it.

Application Synopsis: Do I have brief
descriptions of what each application does?

A brief description of what each application program does. In other words, what is it used for? It is quite possible to set up an electronic spread sheet program to keep track of client billing or do limited property management. It is not difficult to end up with 10 to 15 separate programs. Here is the section to list what all of them are used for.

APPLICATION SYNOPSIS

Name _____
Purpose (word processing, accounting, or whatever)
Operating System
Peripherals Required
Machine Requirements (size of memory or other limitations)
Type of Electronic File (operating system name and limitations, if any)

Run Sheets: Have I laid out the sequence of
steps necessary to operate a particular program?

Each application program should have a separate run sheet. Each sheet shows how to run the program from start to finish. Many programs stand alone; they aren't dependent on any other program having been run. Others require that some other program be run before or after it. This is where you detail it. You may want to use a simple block diagram on the page before your run sheet to show the run sequence, and to highlight the distribution of output.

RUN SHEET

Name of Program _____
Application (brief description of what it does)

How to Initiate (what's required to start it)
Input Required:
Output Required: Printer Specifications
                  Storage Media
Output Expected: Type   Amount
When Run: Time   Frequency

I/O Samples: Have I included all input and output samples with each program?

These are samples of what your programs expect as minimum input and what they give as output. If you have a system that reads bar codes, this is the place to illustrate a bar code. If you are using some form of handwritten entry, this is the place to illustrate it. This is where you would list your voice recognition vocabulary.

With respect to output, your main concern is printed matter. You need examples to show the operator how the printer is set up. Also, if a report comes out missing expected fields, you know something needs to be investigated.

Distribution: Is it clear as to who gets what?

This shows where all the physical output should go. A small computer may run four different systems in a month and produce 20 to 30 reports. The reports or copies may go to people within the business or to people off the premises. Who gets what is a very helpful thing to know.

Often a program will output information to some magnetic storage medium to be used as input at a much later date by some other program. Backup copies of your data files have to be stored somewhere; indicate where.

Electronic File Catalog: Am I keeping track of what data I am putting in what files?

This is simply a list of existing electronic file names with an indication of contents and statuses. Operating systems allow only limited lengths for file names. Six months after you start, it may be difficult to remember the difference between WPMNGRA and WPMNGRB. It is not uncommon for a user to develop 60 to 100 different personal files in a year of working with the system.

Eventually, you will want to start weeding out some of the garbage; this is the purpose of the status indicator. Different information has to be retained for different lengths of time. So, you may want to put a "keep until" date in the status column.

Some application programs allow the generation of file names to store user-created options. Once created, these names cannot be deleted, they can only be replaced. You may want to indicate that these file names are available by putting an asterisk or some other indicator under status.

Glossary: Do I know what everything means?

Your company may use certain words or abbreviations for operating the system in a certain way. You may want to define some common technical terms used in the work and procedures manual itself.

Error Messages: Is it clear what the system is communicating?

Unless you have a totally integrated system, different systems will give different types of responses to certain situations. The operating system may tell you that the disk or disk directory is full. An application program may tell you that you have reached the end of the file. Depending on your familiarity with the program, it is not always apparent what you should do.

Many users and operators like to include copies of the error messages associated with a particular system in the run sheets for that system. It is advisable, however, to keep a complete, updated collection of all messages in one section.

All application programs run under the operating system; therefore, you will usually get operating system messages in addition to program messages. You may have a system built around a data base management system with different application programs written at different times by different people. These programs may access other programs, and so it is advantageous to have a sorted list of all error messages in one place.

Emergency Procedures: Have I covered myself?

Hopefully, you will never have to use this section, but don't count on it. This section should include:

1. The names and telephone numbers of all your hardware suppliers.

2. The names and telephone numbers of all your software suppliers.

3. The names and telephone numbers of two organizations that have the same hardware and operating system as you do. You can search these organizations out by asking the company that sold you the system and by joining user groups in your area. A user group is a pool of potential practical experience. It is often worth having someone in your organization attend the meetings.

4. A reference to your disaster procedures in case of fire, earthquake, or other phenomena of this type.

The User Log: Do I want to keep a diary of system activity?

Some organizations like to keep track of system utilization. You might find that one application package is always being used, whereas another is hardly ever utilized. This might be the basis for adding another terminal or buying an additional small computer and dedicating it to that task.

If a system is utilized in such a way that a great deal of information is distributed, either electronically or physically by hard copy, you need to keep a record to verify that it was both sent and received. Often, the hardware and the software keep track of these and other functions. See that the use statistics collected by the system are adequate for your needs.

The existing system of checks and balances should keep track of your system's paper flow. Just make sure that all your new reports are included. A small business of 15 employees may utilize the services of a part-time bookkeeper. The company may decide to computerize and provide the bookkeeper with new reports. If these reports are produced on Mondays and the bookkeeper comes in on Thursdays, it might be a good idea to keep a document log. Then the operator can initial it upon production of the reports, and the bookkeeper can initial it upon acceptance of the reports. This can be particularly helpful when the document production was done by a part-time employee who doesn't come in on Thursdays.

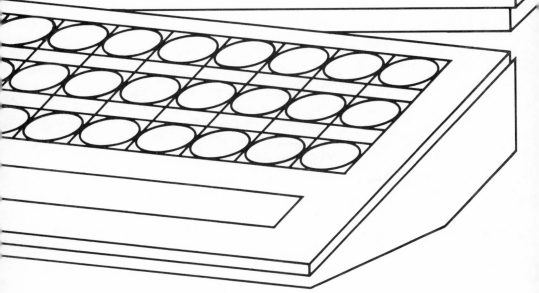

11 PART OF A PROPOSAL FOR A SMALL MANUFAC-TURER

11 PART OF A PROPOSAL FOR A SMALL MANUFACTURER

The following extract is part of a proposal prepared for an actual small research manufacturing company in the electronics industry. The inventory numbers 10,000 separate items. The yearly gross is approximately $1 million. There are approximately 10 full-time employees and 7 part-time employees.

The section marked data processing requirements identifies the particular software packages which meet different needs. For example: the preparation of mailing labels, that is, the printing of the recipient's name and address, is done by a package called "mailing labels." The preparation of letters and reports, on the other hand, needs another package called "word processing."

The section marked Implementation Narrative provides a step-by-step installation plan with associated timings. This is a preliminary in-depth report prepared by a consultant which enables the user to identify the work needed before the computer is installed and also the amount of time it will take for each work module to become functional. The majority of companies will not require this much detail.

The section marked Physical and Personnel Requirements gives a breakdown of these areas and should be self-explanatory.

ABC DATA PROCESSING REQUIREMENTS

8.1 Marketing

    8.1.1   Need: Production of large numbers of mailing labels within different categories.

            Solution: Mailing label software provides 26 categories for selection which can be sorted by zip code, alphabet, or category.

    8.1.2   Need: Production of large numbers of cover letters of individually typewritten quality to be mailed by category.

            Solution: Word processing software allows production of a tailored, standard letter merged according to preselected mailing list categories. Up to 12 variables are available within a standard letter not including the data which is entered at run time.

8.1.3   Need: Customer contact history and analysis:
         (a)   Geographic distribution
         (b)   Advertising efficacy
         (c)   Product distribution
         (d)   Response cycles
         (e)   Sales cycles
         (f)   Support material efficacy

      Solution: Data base management software allows:
         (a)   Information control
         (b)   Record selection
         (c)   Tailored reports
         (d)   Logical selection

8.1.4   Need: Timely data sheets for new products and special orders.

      Solution: Word processing software allows for alphanumeric storage of data sheets on diskettes (external to computer). Information from master can be interchanged, updated, and printed in varying typefaces (including scientific symbols), pitches, and highlights. The system as proposed will produce bar graphs only. Circuit diagrams, engineering drawings, and illustrations must be added by hand.

8.1.5   Need: Technical reports for seminars, publishing, and sales literature.

      Solution: Word processing software. The cycle time from report originator to finished copy can be cut to a third. Once original technical report is on diskette the following changes are possible:

Word, line, sentence, paragraph addition and deletion.

All cutting and pasting functions of the editing process.

All occurrences of a word can be changed by a single command.

Any or all technical sheets in file can be cut and pasted together within the computer to form a new report.

8.2 Administration

    8.2.1 Need: Individual letters. Preparation of quotation proposals.

             Solution: Word processing software. Using ABC letterhead paper, standard information can be computer-generated and added to information entered by clerk.

    8.2.2 Need: Standard letters for:
                    Suppliers
                    Representatives
                    Queries
                    No-bid responses
                    Stockholders
                    Customers
                    Other frequently used alphanumeric documents.

             Solution: Word processing software. Inquirer's name and address and up to 12 variables dropped into standard letter stored on diskette.

    8.2.3 Need: Personnel directory. Consultant directory.

             Solution: Data base management software provides for cross-categorizing of individuals so that a parameter search is possible.

    8.2.4 Need: Sales order summary by week, month, year.

             Solution: Data base management software provides for record fields up to 75 items long with each item discretely named.

    8.2.5 Need: Master price list showing domestic, nonexclusive representation and export prices by quantity.

             Solution: Word processing software.

    8.2.6 Need: Master catalogue of ABC parts and systems.

             Solution: Word processing software.

    8.2.7 Need: In-house inventory control for stationery, forms, printed sales material.

             Solution: Inventory control module software.

8.3 Production

    8.3.1 Need: Parameter search. What parts are available within inventory to meet specific requirements.

             Solution: Data base management software allows the setting

up of data base of parts with characteristics used as variables to determine selection.

8.3.2 Need: Manufacturing inventory.
        Solution: Inventory control module software.

8.3.3 Need: Work-in-progress status report.
        Solution: Data base management software.

8.4 Future possibilities (using BASIC programming language)

8.4.1 Work analysis program

8.4.2 Costing program

8.4.3 Price list change program

8.3.4 Quotation proposal formula program

IMPLEMENTATION NARRATIVE

Upon making the decision to enter into electronic data processing, the following schedule, in order, is a breakdown of the systems analysis that is necessary. (See Figure 21.)

9.1 Analysis

	Hours	**Total**
9.1.1 Mailing labels	5	1–5

1. Analyst meets with all parties concerned.

2. Determine data parameters.

3. Determine information to be included on data base.

4. Determine qualifiers.

5. Determine frequency of lists.

6. Design data record.

7. Document mailing list requirements.

	15	6–20
9.1.2 Inventory		

1. Analyst meets with all parties concerned.

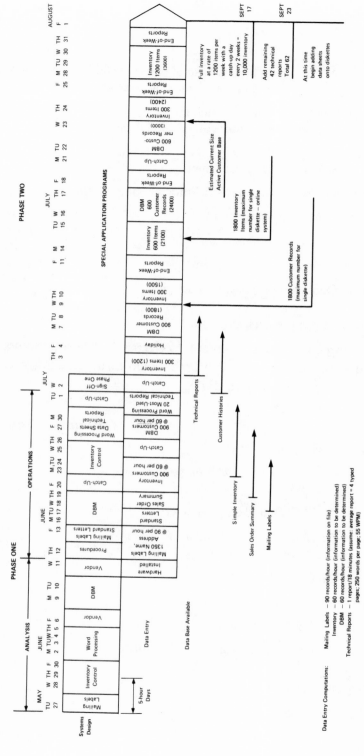

Figure 21

	Hours	**Total**

2. Determine data parameters Item number, description, vendor number/name.

3. Determine information to be included on data base.
   Design an identification numbering system for inventory so that nonproduction items such as stationery might be placed in the 9000 range. Determine online and batch breakdown.

4. Determine qualifiers.
   What reports are to be used. Not all reports are necessary to a company. ABC is unique in that its inventory is so large. Plan online and batch reports.

5. Determine frequency of reports.
   Who wants what, when?
   Necessary for EDP operation planning.

6. Determine requirements for the design of the data record.
   ABC's particular need as determined by all the individuals who come in contact with system.

7. Document inventory control requirements.
   System flowchart.
   Narrative description.
   Report dummies.

9.1.3 Word processing   20   21–40

1. Analyst meets with all parties concerned.

2. Determine standard documents.
   Letters, data sheets, technical reports, price lists, catalogues, forms.

	Hours	**Total**

3. Determine frequency of use.

4. Design an i.d. system to keep track of documents.

5. Determine document use.

6. Document system.

9.1.4 The computer works   5   41–45

1. Arrange training on system configuration to be installed.

2. Work with computer vendor to tailor their software to ABC's needs.

9.1.5 Data base management   10   46–55

1. Analyst meets with all parties concerned.

2. Determine information needed and desired.

   This is crucial to the creation of a data base management system. We might not be able to give everyone everything they want, but if we never allow for it, it means a great deal of work later.

3. Determine security.

   What level of data is available and to whom.

   The computer has both software and hardware locks.

4. Determine frequency of reports.

5. Document system.

9.1.6 The computer vendor   5   56–60

1. Arrange training.

2. Consult with their people.

9.2 Operations

9.2.1 Systems and operations procedures   5   61–65

1. Supervise physical installation.

	Hours	**Total**

2. Set up ABC operating procedures.
   Changing system's date
   Storage of diskettes
   Storage of paper, ribbons, supplies
   Placement of reference manuals
   System's library
   Backup
   How often?
   Stored?

3. Document procedures.

9.2.2	Mailing labels	5	66–70

1. Supervise creation of data base.
   Name/address
   Standard letters

2. Test system.

3. Prepare run book documentation:
   Sample data record
   Qualifiers with explanation
   Sample output
   Operating instruction
   How to run
   What to do in case of error

9.2.3	Data base management	20	71–90

1. Supervise creation of data base.

2. Test system.

3. Prepare run book:
   Data record sample
   Operating instructions

9.2.4	Catch up	5	91–95
9.2.5	Inventory control	20	96–115

1. Design batch and online system:
   It is not possible at this time, because of hardware considerations, to have a 10,000-item real-time system.

	Hours	**Total**

2. Provide operating instructions for individual programs within system:
   Narrative description.
   Sample reports.
   Report distribution.

3. Document system:
   Flowchart
   Input forms
   Inventory i.d. code directory

4. Collect data and oversee entry.

5. Design any necessary forms.

6. Test system.

9.2.6 Word processing—data sheets/technical reports   10   116–125

1. Prepare i.d. system.

2. Supervise creation of data base.

3. Prepare run book and operating instructions.

9.2.7 Catch up   5   126–130

SIGN OFF

PHYSICAL AND PERSONNEL REQUIREMENTS

10.1 Physical requirements

10.1.1 The computer is a 3-part machine composed of
   1 VDT   (occupies single
   1 CPU   desk)
   1 Printer   (stands alone)

   The desk holding the VDT and CPU is   36 inches wide

   (The CPU sits on shelf beneath)   24 inches deep

The operator's chair requires	25 inches depth
The printer on its stand is	23 inches wide
	22 inches deep
The printer in order to run continuous form paper requires an additional	15 inches depth

10.1.2 The work area around the VDT must be kept clear and be available to the operator if work is to be performed efficiently. Data entry records must be kept in order and next to the VDT to facilitate entry.

There must be sufficient clear area so that as a record is entered it can be moved from unentered pile to completed pile easily.

Operation and reference manuals must be easily useable at the VDT.

10.1.3 Storage
A bookshelf is required for the storage of operation and reference manuals.

Magnetic storage media
There is a drawer in the VDT desk that will hold diskettes.

Computer paper will need to be stored.
Much of ABC's work can be produced on standard bond which is already stored.
Inventory reports and some data base management reports may require computer (accordian-fold, continuous) paper.

Extra ribbons and print wheels can be stored in desk.

10.1.4 Possible Configurations (see Figure 22)
The VDT is noiseless. The printer is somewhat noisy.

1. Place the VDT in marketing room with printer on other side of wall in teletype room.

Advantage: Computer is fairly private.
Disadvantage: Printer is not readily accessible. VDT operator may need to reference the printer fairly frequently when setting up word processing runs or doing one-off reports.

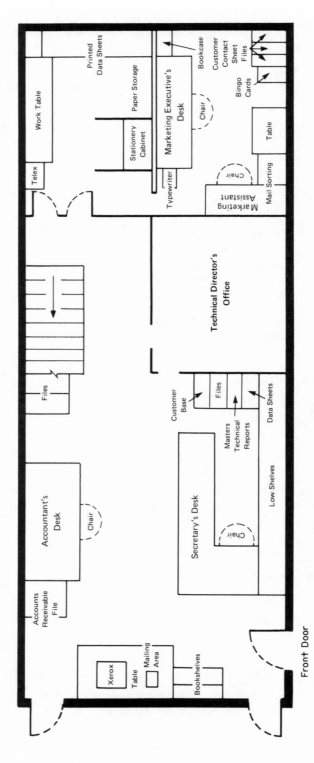

Figure 22 Plan of Top Floor—ABC Inc. (not to scale).

2. Place VDT and CPU in marketing room with printer in same room.

Advantage: Everything is close at hand for the operator.

Disadvantage: The printer is somewhat noisy and particularly on long runs could be disturbing to the occupants.

3. Move part-time accountant into marketing room along with accounts receivable file.
Use accountant's old area for VDT and printer.

Advantage: More spacious area allowing VDT operator better working conditions.

Disadvantage: VDT and printer are in a more public area. There may be a question of data security. However the computer is a physically lockable machine. Also very little of ABC's paper work is of a top secret nature requiring privacy. Finally ABC has few public customers.

10.2 Personnel Requirements.

10.2.1 Existing staff

ABC's current administrative needs are met by:

Clerical assistant	5 h/day
Secretary production assistant	8 h/day
Marketing executive	6 h/day
Marketing assistant	3 h/day
Total	22 h/day

ABC's clerical load is already implying more hours for the marketing assistant.

10.2.2 Duties

Clerical assistant
Operates switchboard
Deals with first level of telephone inquiries
Orders
Requests for information

Does typing
  Letters
  Quotation proposals
Opens, sorts, distributes mail
Does filing
Makes up sales literature packets and sends them out
Does general clerical duties

Secretary/production assistant
  Processes daily accounting forms for part-time accountant
  Takes care of shipping/receiving paper work
  Prepares weekly management reports
  Makes sure special orders are produced
  Does general typing

Marketing executive
  Takes technical sales calls
  Makes telephone sales calls
  Keeps sales literature up to date
  Buys advertising space
  Plans marketing
  Does general typing

Marketing assistant
  Operates switchboard
  Deals with first level of telephone inquiries
    Orders
    Requests for information
  Does typing
    Letters
    Quotation proposals
  Does filing
  Collects and sends out data sheets
  Deals with advertising and bingo card responses

10.2.3 Staff (computer installed):

Electronic data processing (EDP) operator/data entry clerk	3 h/day
Secretary/production assistant	8 h/day
marketing executive	6 h/day
(optional) one data entry clerk	5 h/day

4-day week
June 13–September 23

Assuming 5-day week for regulars,
total is   85 h/week
Data entry clerk   20 h/week

    Total   105 h/week

Divide by 5 for h/day   21 h/day
Existing staff   22 h/day

10.2.4 Duties

The following responsibilities are based on the assumption that a data entry clerk is available. Otherwise the time scale for personnel to attain proficiency and justify the above numbers will be extended.

Data entry clerk—optional
    Enters ABC files onto diskette

EDP operator/data entry clerk
    Operates computer for production runs
    Mailing labels/word processing marketing announcements, advertising—bingo and customer response
    Inventory control
    Data base management weekly reports
    Operates switch board
    Opens, sorts, and distributes mail
    Does filing

Secretary/production assistant
    Processes daily accounting forms for part-time accountant
    Keeps track of shipping and receiving
    Supervises production of special orders
    Supervises data collection for EDP
    Supervises end-of-week report runs

Marketing executive
    Takes customer calls
    Makes sales calls
    Keeps track of sales literature
    Develops new sales literature
    Supervises advertising
    Does market analysis

Note: All persons should be trained to run the computer so that they can substitute for one another.

APPENDIX 1
WHAT COMPUTERS DO NOT DO

1. They do not speak or understand conversational language.
2. They do not train themselves.
3. They do not organize data without outside help.
4. They do not know, most of the time, when things go wrong mechanically, electronically, or programmatically.

APPENDIX 2
RULES OF THUMB

1. The number of typed pages per single-density 5¼-inch disk is about   25 to 35 pages

2. The number of typed pages per single-density 8-inch disk is about   100 to 140 pages

3. 100 kbytes is about   24 pages

4. A single-density 5¼-inch disk holds approximately 300 records of about 250 characters each. This is very much a guestimate. There are too many variables to arrive at an accurate figure. Use this as a place to start.

5. Disk space: unformatted. (Formatted you have less.)

5¼-inch	
Single-density	128 kbytes
Double-density	356 kbytes
8-inch	
Single-density	400 kbytes
Double-density	800 kbytes

6. Word processing data entry times:
To enter original material, about   100 lines/hour
To do repetitive typing, about   200 lines/hour
To do revision typing, about   150 lines/hour

7. Time to print a report of 150 records prepared from a base of 200, some computing and formatting, no spooling, dot-matrix printer, about   10 to 15 minutes

8. Approximate time to sort 1000 records   1 hour

9. Approximate time to write 25 lines of working
code   1 day

10. Approximate time to write simple accounts receivable analysis   20 to 50 hours
program   50 to 200 hours

11. Average number of lines of code to compute a
principal and interest payment and to take care
of all the possible computation and data entry
exceptions   125 lines

12. Average number of lines of code to find a
particular record, including the exception routines   100 lines

IF YOU GET BETTER RESULTS THAN THESE FIGURES CONSIDER IT A
BONUS.

IF YOU GET WORSE REMEMBER THAT THESE FIGURES ARE CALLED
RULES OF THUMB FOR A REASON.

APPENDIX 3
SYSTEM SPECIFICATIONS

1. Name of system—brief narrative of what it does

2. Current problems

3. Objectives
   a. Mathematical operations required
   b. Processing required

4. Constraints

5. Existing equipment—what requirements it imposes

6. Samples of required reports
   a. Attached
   b. See _____ (location) _____

QUESTIONS TO ASK
WHEN LOOKING FOR A COMPUTER

1. What packages are available **now**?

2. Is there any additional software required by the packages in order to run properly, such as a particular language?

3. Has someone from the business reviewed the software?

4. What is the operating system?

5. What amount of internal memory is needed to run the software?

6. What is the price of the basic system to handle the above?

7. What support can be expected for this price?

8. What training is offered in this price?

9. Can additional devices be added easily?

10. Is the system easy to use?

11. How many jobs/tasks can be run at the same time?

12. How much online storage is there?

13. How many people can use the machine at the same time?

NOTE: If you are just starting out the answers will give you some indication of the kind of machine you are looking at.
If you have done the analysis you know what answers are necessary to meet your needs.

APPENDIX 5
STEPS INVOLVED IN PROGRAMMING

1. Determine the input and output required. Have or make samples of all expected reports.

2. Do a rough design of the program.

3. Work out the logic.

4. Write the code.

5. Test the code and debug it.

6. Document the finished program.

GLOSSARY

ACOUSTIC COUPLER   A device which cradles a telephone receiver so that information may be sent over the telephone line. See modem.

ALGORITHM   The logical steps required to solve a problem. See *Programmer.*

APPLESOFT BASIC   A particular dialect of the BASIC programming language.

APPLICATION PACKAGE   A collection of documented programs that enables hardware to be put to a particular use. Payroll and word processing are examples.

APPLICATION PROGRAM   A set of instructions that utilizes the computer for a practical purpose.

ASCII   American standard code for information interchange (pronounced ass-key.) A way of representing information in binary form.

ASSEMBLY LANGUAGE   A set of programming symbols that links directly to the operation codes of a machine; a low-level language.

ASYNCHRONOUS   When used with data transmission, usually refers to the sending of data one character at a time. The data uses its own start and stop information and is therefore not synchronous with the time base of the main machine. Most commonly used in slower-speed human-operated terminals.

AUDIT TRAILS   Information stored to indicate the passage of data through a system.

AVERAGE ACCESS TIME   How long it takes a device to get a single piece of data.

BACKUP   Copies of a complete, current set of data used as protection against loss.

BANK SELECT   A method of accessing additional memory. Additional

206

memory is available in discrete amounts; each amount is a bank that is chosen or selected by the operating system.

BAR CODE   Machine-printed stripes that represent information, usually numerical. Used in point of sale for marking the price of goods.

BASIC   beginner's all-purpose symbolic instruction code. A programming language popular for use with small computers. A high-level language, fairly easy to learn but hard to use well.

BAUD RATE   The signaling speed of a communication channel. The number of times the state of a line changes per second, which is equal to the bit rate when each signal element equals one bit of information.

BENCHMARK   A point of reference from which measurements can be made.

BIDIRECTIONAL   The ability to operate in both directions, usually in reference to printers. (The bidirectional printer is faster.)

BITS   A measure of computer information, which is stored as a two-state representation. Something is either on or off, either a 0 or a 1. These two digits, called BInary digiTS, give the abbreviation BITS.

BLACK BOX   A symbolic device that takes in raw material and gives out a finished product.

BOILER PLATE   Used in word processing to mean standard information. "At the end of the page, put in the usual boiler plate paragraph about the company."

BOOT   Contraction of bootstrap. A process in which a small built-in program is used to load others. "When you turn on the machine it will boot the program in disk drive A."

BUFFER   A temporary storage area to hold information that eventually goes to the processor or to the I/O devices. Exists to accommodate different rates of data transfer or production.

BUG   An error in logic; can refer to either hardware or software.

BURN-IN PERIOD   The shake-down period during which all hardware elements are continuously powered. Designed to force any weak parts to fail before the system goes into actual use.

BUS   The communication junction for the lines that transmit functionally grouped signals within a computer. There are three types of buses: data, address, and control.

BUSINESS PACKAGES   Program packages specific to business use as opposed to scientific use.

BYTE   A storage segment large enough to hold one character. "This machine uses 8 bits to hold the alphanumeric symbol 'A'."

CALENDAR METHOD   A method of taking backup in which a duplicate data base is assigned a particular time slot.

CANNED PROGRAMS   Prewritten programs.

CAPACITY   The memory size of any device that holds data.

CARD READERS   Devices that accept information in the form of a punched or marked card.

CATHODE RAY TUBES   Refers to the television-like screen of a computer abbreviated CRT. Originally all screens used CRT technology. Now the term VDT has replaced it, unless a specific reference to this type of device is meant.

COBOL   common business oriented language. A high-level programming language.

CODE   The actual instructions written in a particular programming language.

COLD START   Starting a machine from a power-off state. See *Warm Start*.

COMPRESSED (PRINT)   A printer feature allowing it to print narrower characters in the same width. Enables an 80-column printer to squeeze 132 characters into 80 columns.

CONFIGURE   To arrange the elements of a computer system into a working whole.

CONNECTORS   Mechanical devices that enable paths for electricity to be attached to one another.

CONTROLLER   When used with reference to an external storage device, the hardware mechanism with its built-in software that handles I/O areas.

CP/M   An operating system written by Digital Research for 8080- and Z80-based microcomputers. CP/M is an abbreviation for Control Program Monitor.

CPS   characters per second. Used when referring to a printer's print speed.

CPU   central processing unit. The heart of a computer system which does the essential data manipulation, mathematical and logical, of the device called a computer.

CRT   See *Cathode Ray Tubes*.

DAISY CHAIN   Peripheral devices connected together sequentially in a round robin fashion.

DATA   Plural formation of datum. Physical symbols to indicate the basic elements of information.

DATA ACQUISITION   The gathering of information by a computer system in a form that is understandable by the unit utilizing it.

DATA BASE   The specific collection of cross-referenced elements used by a system.

DATA BASE MANAGEMENT   The use of a system to control the flow of information elements.

DATA BASE MANAGEMENT SYSTEM   Specifically, the software which enables a computer to manage information elements.

DEBUG   To track down an error in logic.

DECISION CHARTS   Flowcharts or other types of tabular diagrams which represent logical consequences.

DECISION TABLES   A rectangular grid made of four smaller rectangles used to lay out actions and assorted conditions.

DEFINING FIELDS   Specifying the type of information that will be acceptable as the individual data value.

DESCENDERS   The segment of an alphabetic character that extends below the horizontal. "p", "g", and "q" all have descenders. Descenders make lowercase letters easier to read.

DIGITIZER   A device that turns analog signals into numeric equivalents.

DIP SWITCH   A dual in-line package often found on printers consisting of small hardware switches that have to be manually set. Set up on the configuration of a system and not normally changed.

DISK   A form of external storage that can be accessed directly.

DISK DRIVE   The machine that reads from and writes to a disk.

DISTRIBUTION CHART   A diagram that specifies the destination of printed output of a computer system.

DMA   direct memory access. Information is routed directly from the memory location to a device without requiring intermediary manipulation by the CPU. Some types of video display terminals use DMA.

DOCUMENTATION   Humanly understandable records of how a computer system operates and the logic of its design.

DOT-MATRIX PRINTER   A printer that forms symbols by the use of dots in a pattern. See letter quality.

DOUBLE (DUAL) DENSITY   Refers to disks on which twice the information is packed in the same space as the disk originally held.

DOUBLE (DUAL) SIDED   Refers to disks where both sides are used to store information.

DOWN   The computer system has ceased functioning.

ELECTRONIC FILING SYSTEMS   Programs that enable the user to store, file, sort, and do minor manipulation of data.

ELECTRONIC MAIL   The terminal/computer is used like a mail service to send information to someone who has access to a terminal/computer.

ELECTRONIC SPREAD SHEETS   Programs that enable the user to lay out information in rows and columns that can be related by mathematical formulas.

EMULATE   One type of system operates as though it were another type of system.

ENCRYPTION   The altering of information so that it is unintelligible to anyone without the proper conversion key.

END USER   The person who has final employment for the results of the computer system's processing.

ERROR CONDITION   An indication for the system that things are not what they should be within its operating subsystems.

ERROR MESSAGE   An error condition communicated by the system to the human user.

FIELD   Individual data values within a file. "Last name" is a field within a file.

FIFO   first in first out. In a post office queue, the first person is served and then the next in order of entry into the queue.

FILE   A collection of stored data.

FILE PROTECTION   Electronic or mechanical means of ensuring that a file is not accidentally erased.

FIRMWARE   Software embedded in hardware.

THE FIRST-TIME RULE   Things are never quite the same as the very first time something is done.

FLOPPY DISK   Auxiliary storage device. A thin, nonrigid magnetic disk in a square supporting envelope.

FLOWCHARTS   The graphic representation of an algorithm.

FORMAT   The specific form and style the data takes.

FORMATTED   Printed text that has been put into final form and disks that have been prepared to accept data are considered to be formatted.

FORTRAN   formula translation. A language designed for complex numerical calculations; not efficient for most business applications.

FRICTION FEED   Paper is held in and fed through a printer by force of contact.

FUNCTION CHARTS   Diagrams showing who or what does what in a system.

GANNT CHART   A bar chart showing the stages of a project in relation to time; named after one of its originators.

GIGO   garbage in garbage out. No matter how good the program or the equipment, what you get out is only as good as what you put in.

GRANDPARENT METHOD   A system of taking backup. Copies of the data base exist for three generations; the oldest is purged in the fourth cycle.

GRAPHICS   The input to and/or output from a computer of picture data.

GREEN PHOSPHOR   A chemical used in video terminals to give green characters on a dark background.

HANDSHAKING   Communication between equipment to indicate their send-and-receive statuses.

HARD DISK   External auxiliary storage. Magnetic disks in a hermetically sealed box.

HARD-SECTORED DISK   Floppy disks that are mechanically formatted.

HARDWARE   The physical stuff of a computer.

HEADER RECORDS   Preliminary records that identify a file.

HIERARCHY   A collection arranged into a series by precedence.

HIGH-LEVEL LANGUAGE   A set of computer instructions easily under-stood by humans. A computer requires that a program written in a high-level language be translated before it can run the instructions. See *Low-Level Language*.

HIRES   high resolution. This refers to the picture quality of the display terminal.

HOUSEKEEPING   The necessary steps to keep a system functional.

I/O   input-output. A term used to describe a device or state. The operating system controls the I/O.

I/O DESCRIPTOR SHEET   Documentation that describes in specific terms the type of input and output data a computer system expects.

I/O DEVICES   Equipment that handles data either going into or coming out of a central processing unit. A device may be input only, output only, or input and output.

IMPACT   This refers to a method of printing where a mechanical letter is hit by a hammerlike device.

INDEX   To use the same field or fields from a collection of records to reference the locations of the entire record.

INDEXING   Creating a small file of fields that reference the file of whole records.

INFORMATION FLOW   The path that data takes in progressing through a system.

INITIALIZE   Procedures required to set up equipment for acceptance of data. Soft disks often have to be initialized before they can accept data. (Some operating systems use the term formatting to mean initializing the disk.)

INSTALLATION INSTRUCTIONS   A collection of humanly understand-able procedures on how to set up computer hardware and/or software and make it operational.

INTEGER BASIC   A dialect of BASIC.

INTELLIGENT   An I/O device is considered intelligent when it can do part of the data processing independently of the main computer.

INTERFACE   The area where two systems meet and act upon one another.

INTERFACE CARD   A printed circuit card that plugs into a computer and enables it to talk to peripheral devices.

INTERRUPTS   Signals that stop normal program flow and demand attention.

ISAM   index sequential address method. A random-access method for storing and retrieving records on devices that can read and write information directly to a specific address.

K (KILO)   A measure of storage capacity roughly equivalent to 1000. Because computer addresses are stored by binary digits, the value of K is 2^n, so 2^{10} is 1024. For general purposes the figure 1000 is used.

KEY   The field or fields used in a record to uniquely identify it. This enables software to sort or select the records by key rather than dealing with the whole record.

KEYBOARD   The typewriter-like collection of keys that enables information to be entered into the computer.

THE LAST-TIME RULE   The last time is different from every other time.

LATENCY TIME   The rotational delay in reading to or writing from a direct-access memory device. If the information requested has just passed under the read head, then the latency time is the waiting period until the information again rotates under the head.

LETTER QUALITY   Fully formed print characters. The printed result looks as if it has been printed on an electric typewriter.

LOGO   A computer language initially designed for teaching children programming.

LOW-LEVEL LANGUAGE   A set of computer instructions easily understood by the machine. Programs written in low-level language are fast and efficient for the machine but they are difficult for humans to understand and write. See *High-Level Language.*

M (MEGA)   One million.

MAGNETIC MEDIA   Usually refers to disks and tapes, because these devices are made up of an inert base with a coating that is sensitive to changes in a magnetic field.

MAIL MERGE   Inserting names and addresses into material prepared by a word processor.

MAIL PROGRAMS   Application programs that enable you to store name and address lists so that you can generate mailing labels according to specific criteria.

MAINFRAMES   Large computers. Airlines use mainframes to handle passenger bookings.

MEGABYTE   1 million bytes (Abbreviated MB).

MEMORY   The area of information storage within a computer. Specifically refers to storage that is under direct electronic access by the CPU without any mechanical intermediary.

MEMORY TYPEWRITER   A typewriter with electronic memory storage capacity.

MENU   A list of choices presented on the VDT by a program to the user of the computer system. One menu may lead to several others. Such interactive programs are called menu driven.

MHz   megahertz. One million cycles per second. A unit of measurement used to talk about the speed of a computer chip. A microchip of 8 MHz is faster than one of 2 MHz.

MICROCOMPUTER   A small computer.

MICROFICHE   Film the size of an index card upon which documents that have been reduced photographically are stored. There is no direct connection between microfiche and microcomputers.

MICROFILM   A roll of film upon which documents that have been reduced photographically are stored. There is no direct connection between microfilm and microcomputers.

MINI   A computer that is more powerful than a small computer but not as powerful as a mainframe.

MODEM   A device that enables computer equipment to talk over telephone lines. The digital signal of a computer has to be MOdulated to go over the voice line and DEModulated back into digital signals for the computer equipment.

MODULE   A self-contained segment that is part of a larger whole. Hardware can be modular in design and so can software.

MONITOR   A television screen-like device with greater picture definition.

MOTHER BOARD   Contains the main electronic circuitry of a computer. It implies that other peripheral boards can be "slotted" onto it.

MPU   microprocessing unit.

MTBF   mean time between failures.

MULTIPROCESSOR   A computer with more than one CPU. Effectively each user of the system has their own computer.

MULTITASKING   The CPU does more than one thing during a single work cycle. It does this by splitting the cycle into smaller time units and working on each job for part of the cycle.

MULTIUSER   A computer system which allows more than one individual to utilize the system at a given time.

MURPHY'S LAW   Anything that can go wrong will. Attributed to the first person to observe that buttered bread always falls face down.

NANOSECOND   One billionth of a second.

NARRATIVE DESCRIPTION   The human-language description of the steps involved in a particular job.

NETWORK   Two or more computers used together to process information.

NETWORK COMMUNICATION PACKAGES   Software that enables different computers to work together.

OCR   optical character reader. A device that uses light to read preprinted alphanumeric information into a computer.

OEM   original equipment manufacturer. A manufacturer who adds value to a product before selling it to the final user.

OFF THE SHELF   Prepackaged software that can be purchased (gotten "off the shelf").

ONLINE   To be in direct communication with the CPU.

OPERATING SYSTEM   Software that acts as the traffic cop in a computer system; it runs the computer. (As opposed to application programs which run the system.)

OPTICAL CHARACTER READERS   See OCR.

PACKAGE   A prewritten program designed to perform a specific function.

PARALLEL   Side by side. Used mainly to refer to the transmission of data. If 8 bits of information are sent in parallel then 8 physical wires or lines of communication are carrying the data.

PARALLEL TESTING   Running the new system alongside the old system in actual operation, using real data, and comparing the results.

PASCAL   A high-level structured language. Comparatively easy to use and maintain for an experienced programmer.

PERIPHERAL DEVICES   Equipment used by the central processing unit but physically separate from it.

PERT   project evaluation and review technique. A management technique to plan and control complex projects.

PIXEL   The element that makes up a digital picture. The more elements the sharper the picture. Often used when talking of VDT screens.

PL/1   A high-level structured language often used for system development.

PLOTTERS   Output devices that allow the computer to draw lines on paper.

PLUG COMPATIBLE   Equipment built by one manufacturer that can be mechanically connected to another manufacturer's equipment and operate without modification.

PORTS   The logical connection through which data is transferred under CPU control. A serially operated printer must be connected to the serial port.

POWERING DOWN   Turning off a computer system. Because the system may be made up of many different devices, power may have to be turned on or off separately and in some kind of order.

POWERING UP   Turning on a computer system. See powering down.

PRINTERS   Output devices that allow the computer to write letters, numbers, and special characters on paper.

PROCESSING DEVICES   Electronic chips that manipulate data logically and/or arithmetically.

PROGRAM GENERATORS   Theoretically, programs that ask the user a number of questions and, depending on the answers, result in an application program.

PROGRAMMER   An individual who translates an algorithm, the steps to perform a function, into the specific language of a computer. Programmers write the directions that tell computers what to do.

PROJECT MANAGEMENT   The controls used to ensure that tasks are completed correctly and on time.

PROM   programmable read-only memory. A type of chip.

PROTOCOL   The code of behavior that must be followed in order to set results. Different computer networks have different protocols that must be used, and not all hardware and software can use all protocols.

QUEUING   Waiting in line. Devices or data often have to wait in line to be operated on.

RAM   random access memory. A chip that has individually addressable storage locations.

READ-ONLY STORAGE   A device which can only be read from, not written to.

READ-WRITE STORAGE   A device which can be read from and/or written to.

REAL-TIME CLOCK   A device within a computer system which keeps track of the time of day. It is used for date stamping.

REASONABLENESS   Information to be entered into a computer system has to fall within certain predetermined parameters. All inventory numbers are in the 9000 range.

REBOOT   To bring up a program again. See *Boot*.

RECORD   A collection of related data fields on a particular subject.

RECORD LOCK   A software device to prevent unauthorized use of a record.

ROM   read-only memory.

RS232C   A binary serial bus standard. Frequently used with CRT terminals and slow printers.

RUN   The execution of a program.

RUN CHART   The diagram that illustrates the operating steps for using a computer system.

RUN SHEETS   Documentation that details how to run specific sets of programs on a computer system.

S100   A 100-line bus for connecting the 8080, 8085, and Z80 family of chips to external devices, a standard type in the small computer world.

SCREENS   The information that appears on the window of a VDT at any one time.

SCROLLING   Moving the data up and down through the window of a VDT.

SEARCH KEY   The field(s) on which records have been organized for fast retrieval of specific data elements. "The distribution report uses the zip code as the search key of the vendor file."

SERIAL   Arranged in a series. Usually refers to the transmission of data. Data is transmitted serially because there may only be a single path as in the read-write head of a disk drive, or a single conductor cable as to a VDT.

SERIAL DATA   Data that has been arranged in rows to make up packets of information. The letters N, A, M, E sent one after the other (serially) make up a word.

SINGLE-ACCESS   Dealing with one situation at a time.

SINGLE-SIDED   A disk can only be read to or written from one surface.

SINGLE USER   A computer that can only be used by one individual at a time.

6502   The manufacturer's identification number for a common micro-processor chip.

SMART   See *Intelligent*.

SOFT-SECTORED DISK   The disk is formatted by a program that magnetically determines the areas to accept information. A soft-sectored disk can be formatted in different ways by different operating systems. A hard disk does not have that option.

SOFT SWITCH   An electronic switch that does not require outside mechanical intervention.

SOFTWARE   Programs; the written instructions that tell a computer what to do. Formed from the word hardware.

SPLIT SCREEN   The VDT is progammatically divided to show different information at the same time. A word processor that has split-screen capability can show information from the current file and also from other files of your choice.

SPOOLING   simultaneous peripheral operations on line. A method of handling slow I/O devices by putting the data to be transferred into a hold area.

STATUS LINE   The top or bottom line on a VDT that shows current information about the state of the processing.

STORAGE DEVICES   Any equipment that retains coded information that can be accessed by the central processing unit.

SURGE SUPPRESSOR   A device to smooth out fluctuations on the power line that feeds the computer.

SWITCHING BOX   A device that enables multiple pieces of equipment to be attached to a single port.

SYNERGY   Two or more things working together. Together they are more efficient than they are separately.

SYSTEM ARCHITECTURE   The basic design of the hardware of a computer.

SYSTEM HOUSE   An establishment that designs or implements software for business systems.

SYSTEMS ANALYSIS   The field of study that is concerned with humans and machines performing specific jobs. Specifically utilizes electronic data processing equipment.

SYSTEMS UTILITIES   Programs that help the computer control the way it uses programs.

TAPE   Magnetic storage tape; stores information sequentially and is used mainly with small computers as a form of backup storage.

TELECOMMUNICATIONS   The exchange of information at a distance, using cable, telephone, radio, or any other medium to move the information.

TERMINAL   Devices that allow data processor users to interact with a computer's I/O in an immediate manner. The majority of terminals currently have a keyboard and a view screen.

TEXT EDITOR   Software that allows you to manipulate inputted alphanumeric data. Enables the user to "create" text.

TEXT FORMATTER   Software that allows you to manipulate outputted alphanumeric data. Enables the user to "layout" text.

THEORY OF EXTREMES   The minimum and maximum states of something.

THROUGHPUT   The average amount of time for a computer system to complete a job from start to finish.

TIME FRAME   The boundaries of a measured period.

TIMESHARE   At the user level this means a number of different users buying and sharing time on a large computer. When referring to hardware it means sharing time on the CPU.

TOUCH PAD   A device that registers pressure and converts it to electrical information.

TOUCH-SENSITIVE   A device that is responsive to human touch.

TRACTOR   A device on a printer that engages the holes in continuous paper and helps feed it through the machine.

TRAILER RECORDS   Data records at the end of a file that contain summary information about the file.

TRANSIENTS   A source of electrical power trouble. "Spikes" of power that can upset hardware and software.

TRANSMISSION   The sending of data from one device to another.

TURNKEY SYSTEM   A computer system in which the hardware begins operating the application system as soon as the power is turned on. The system is easy enough to be operated by an inexperienced computer user.

TYPEWRITER INTERFACES   Devices that enable a small computer to use an electric or electronic typewriter as an online printer.

UNIX   An operating system designed by Bell Laboratories. The language C is part of this system.

UPGRADE   To update computer hardware by adding devices that make the machine larger or faster or better.

USER-FRIENDLY   Able to be utilized by someone with no computer experience.

USER LOG   A diary of who used the system, when, and why.

VDT   Video display terminal.

VIDEO DISKS   Disks that store pictures as information. Currently they are read-only devices and are just beginning to be used with small computers.

VOICE RECOGNITION   The ability of a computer system to understand spoken human words and to act on them.

WAND   An operational input device that reads bar code. It fits in the user's hand like a pencil.

WARM START   Returning the computer to its initial start-up state, without interrupting the power supply. Data will be cleared from memory.

WINCHESTER   The name applied to the technology used in most hard disk drives. It is the original hard disk technology which is used with small computers.

WISH LIST   The collection of things most wanted. It helps you define what you are after.

WORD PROCESSING   The ability of a system to create alphanumeric text, manipulate the text, and print it out according to design. Word processing requires both a text editor and a text formatter.

WORK AND PROCEDURES MANUAL   A manual of documentation about the application of the computer system. It tells the user what is needed to run the programs.

WORK SAMPLING   Studying the complete business process by looking at a representative part.

WRITE-PROTECTED   Insuring that stored information cannot be accidentally erased by being written over with new information.

Z80   Manufacturer's identification for a common microprocessor chip.

INDEX